广东省交通运输厅　主编

蔚蓝船说

—— 广东商船船型变迁

21世纪海上丝绸之路与广东航运丛书 二

广东旅游出版社

中国·广州

图书在版编目（CIP）数据

蔚蓝船说：广东商船船型变迁 / 广东省交通运输厅主编. — 广州：广东旅游出版社，2017.11

（21世纪海上丝绸之路与广东航运丛书；2）

ISBN 978-7-5570-1145-1

Ⅰ. ①蔚… Ⅱ. ①广… Ⅲ. ①民用船－船型－交通运输史－广东 Ⅳ. ①F552.9

中国版本图书馆CIP数据核字（2017）第253943号

出 版 人：刘志松
策划编辑：官　顺
责任编辑：厉颖卿
装帧设计：谢晓丹
责任校对：李瑞苑
责任技编：刘振华

蔚蓝船说：广东商船船型变迁
WEILAN CHUANSHUO: GUANGDONG SHANGCHUAN CHUANXING BIANQIAN

出版发行：广东旅游出版社
社　　址：广州市越秀区环市东路338号银政大厦西楼12楼
邮　　编：510060
邮购电话：020-87348243
网　　址：广东旅游出版社网站：www.tourpress.cn
印　　刷：佛山市华禹彩印有限公司印刷
　　　　　（佛山市南海区罗村联合工业区西二区三路1-1号）
开　　本：787毫米×1092毫米　　1/16
印　　张：12
字　　数：150千字
版　　次：2017年11月第1版
印　　次：2017年11月第1次印刷
印　　数：1-2000册
定　　价：88.00元

版权所有　侵权必究

本书如有错页倒装等质量问题，请直接与印刷厂联系换书。

《蔚蓝船说：广东商船船型变迁》
编委会

主 任
李静

（广东省交通运输厅厅长）

Director: Li Jing

副主任
刘晓华

（广东省交通集团总经理，时任广东省交通运输厅副厅长）

Deputy director: Liu Xiaohua

编委（以姓氏笔画为序）
The Editoroal Board：(in order of strokes of Chinese characters)

付伦香　袁炎清　王立文　文艺　付广　余灵　何国卫　陈建平　汪健
林镇钦　金行德　郑勤　杨桦　余曼平　聂昌琪　梁金科　童本标

Fu Lunxiang　Yuan Yanqing　Wang Liwen　Wen Yi　Fu Guang　Yu Ling
He Guowei　Chen Jianping　Wang Jian　Lin Zhenqin　Jin Xingde　Zheng Qin
Yang Hua　Yu Manping　Nie Changqi　Liang Jinke　Tong Benbiao

序

广东自古就有很强的造船、航海能力，以及海外贸易传统，是经济大省、外贸大省，也是海洋大省、文化大省。从史前珠海的岩画，西汉南越王陵墓提筒纹饰的船纹，汉代的独木舟、木板船模、陶船模，东晋的八槽舰，到唐宋时的木兰舟、大战船，再到明后期的中国四大船型之一的"广船"，明清时代广东更在中国造船史上书写下了辉煌的一页。

鸦片战争爆发后，西方列强对中国开始了瓜分和掠夺，中国逐步沦为半封建半殖民地国家。欧美资本主义国家的商船，相继涌入珠江水域，控制珠江航运，广东的海外贸易航线逐渐受排挤。新中国成立后，处于停滞状态的民族工业亟待恢复和发展，造船工业不仅关系到国民经济发展，更是海洋发展的重要支柱产业。广东商船也深深打上了这个时代的烙印。

改革开放以来，我国进入了新的发展时期，国家实力迅速增强。广东商船逐步从封闭走向开放，立足国内，面向世界，不断扩大与世界航运和造船界的交往，面貌发生了巨大变化，取得了显著成就。新世纪以来，中国造船工业得到快速发展，2010年，中国造船份额位列世界第一位，已能够自主设计建造30万吨级超大型原油船和8000箱级超大型集装箱船，并已成功进入液化天然气船建造市场，打破了少数国家的垄断。目前，除豪华游船等少数船型外，中国已经能够建造符合各种国际规范、航行于任何海域的船舶。作为中国三大造船基地之一，广东的造船业呈现出良好的发展势头。

21世纪是海洋世纪，海洋在全球的战略地位日益突出，海洋经济已成为世界经济发展的新领域、新趋向。党的十八大作出了建设"海洋强国"重大战略决策，实施"一带一路"发展战略，广东积极融入"21世纪海上丝绸之路""粤港澳大湾区"建设，加强广东自贸试验区发展、打造"海洋强省"，广东与"海上丝绸之路"沿线经济体的经贸交流不断深化，广东已成为"21世纪海上丝绸之路"沿线的重要节点和建设"21世纪海上丝绸之路"的重要"桥头堡"。在这个进程中，航运业将扮演越来越重要的角色，需要更全面地谋划广东航运业的建设和发展。

《蔚蓝传说——广东商船船型变迁》的编辑出版，有助于固化、沉淀广东商船船型发展的历史文化，推动广东航运、贸易的进步，进一步促进广东社会经济发展，为建设"21世纪海上丝绸之路"贡献力量！

梁建伟
（广东省人民政府参事、广东海事局原局长）

Preface

Guangdong has a very strong ability of traditional shipbuilding, marine and overseas trade, which makes it a marine cultural province. From the prehistoric rock paintings in Zhuhai, Nanyue King Mausoleum bin decoration ship lines, wooden boats, canoes, boats pottery of Han Dynasty, the Eastern Jin Dynasty to the Tang Dynasties waterlight cabin, the war ship, boat Mulan, and then to one of China's four major ship "Guangdong shipyard" in late Ming dynasty, especially in the Ming and Qing dynasty, Guangdong ship wrote a brilliant page in Chinese shipbuilding history.

After the outbreak of the Opium War, imperialist powers began to divide and plunder China, and it gradually reduced to a semi-colonial and semi-feudal country. Merchant ships of European and American capitalist countries poured into the Pearl River waters, and controlled the Pearl River shipping. Guangdong overseas trade routes were excluded gradually. After the founding of new China, the state industry in a stagnant state needs to be restored and developed. The shipbuilding industry was not only related to the national economic development, but also an important pillar industry for marine development. Guangdong Merchant was also deeply marked with the imprint of this era.

Since the reform and opening-up, China has entered into a new period of development, in which the national strength increased rapidly. Guangdong merchants gradually got open from closed situation, based on the domestic, facing the world, and expanding contacts with world shipping and shipbuilding industry which led it to a new face and great achievements. Since the new century, Chinese shipbuilding industry has developed rapidly. In 2010, China's shipbuilding share was ranked first in the world. China can design and build 300,000-ton super-large crude oil tankers and 8000-class super-large container ships. Moreover, China went into the liquefied natural gas ship construction market, which broke the monopoly of some countries. At present, except for some luxury cruise ships, China has been able to build ships that can match all kinds of international norms and sail in any sea areas. As one of the China's three major shipbuilding bases, Guangdong's shipbuilding industry shows a good momentum of development.

The 21st century is the ocean century. The marine strategic position in the world has become increasingly prominent, and the marine economy has become a new world of economic development, new trends. The 18th National Congress of the Communist Party of China made a major strategic decision to build a "marine power", and implemented "The Belt and Road" development strategy. Guangdong actively integrated into the construction of "21st Century Maritime Silk Road" and "Guangdong-Hong Kong-Macao Greater Bay" by strengthening the development of Guangdong Free Trade Zone and building a "marine strong"province. Economic communication between Guangdong and areas along the "Maritime Silk Road" continues to deepen, and Guangdong plays an important role in the construction of it. In this process, the shipping industry becomes more and more important, for which the development and construction of it needs to be planned more comprehensively.

The publishing of this album helps to make the history and culture of Guangdong merchant ship development become more solid and precipitate. It will promote the improvement of shipping and trade in Guangdong, and moreover promote the social and economic development in Guangdong. This album will definitely contribute to the construction of "21st century Maritime Silk Road".

目 录

001　上篇　海上丝绸之路与广东商船 >

004　第一章　古代海上丝绸之路与广东商船

014　第二章　21世纪海上丝绸之路，广船再出发

014　共同建设"21世纪海上丝绸之路"　Jointly build "21st-century Maritime Silk Road"

017　新世纪机遇　Opportunities in the new century

019　中篇　图说广东商船船型变迁 >

021　第一章　古代广东商船船型（1840年以前）

022　广东最古老的船舶记载　Records of the oldest ships in Guangdong

024　独木舟　The canoe

025　古战船——南越王船　Ancient warship - Nan Yue Boat

026　西汉木板船　Wooden ship in the Western Han Dynasty

026　东汉陶船模　Pottery ship in the Eastern Han Dynasty

027　八槽舰　Eight boat ship

028　唐代战船与民船　The warship and privateers in the Tang Dynasty

029　宋元大航海时代　Navigation Era in the Song and Yuan Dynasties

031　明清大海船与大航海时代同时到来　The advent of large ships and navigation era in the Ming and Qing Dynasties

035　清代是广东商船最辉煌时代　The Qing Dynasty: the most brilliant time of Guangdong merchant ships

042　第二章　近代商船运输船型（1840—1949年）

044　第一艘到达欧美的中国木帆船 Chinese Wooden masted boat: the first ship arrived in Europe and the United States

046　中国最后一艘三桅古帆船 The last Chinese ancient sailing ship

047　广东民俗——广东花尾渡 Guangdong folk - Hua Wei ferry

050　第一艘来自欧洲的汽轮船 The first steam ship from Europe

050　我国第一艘蒸汽机轮船 China's first steam engine ship

052　19世纪60年代"中国最大的石船坞" "China Largest Stone Dock" in 1860's

053　洋商洋船的年代 The age of the foreign merchant ships

057　第三章　现代广东商船船型（1949年至今）

057　艰苦创业——改革开放前 The start-up – before the reform and opening up

065　扬帆起航——改革开放20年 Sailing – 20 years of the reform and opening-up

071　驶向大海——进入新世纪 To the sea – enter into the new century

076　第四章　珠江船型变迁

076　广州珠江 Guangzhou Pearl River

080　海珠桥 Haizhu Bridge

083　大沙头与太古仓码头 Da Sha Tou and Tai Gu Cang Wharf

086　珠江轮渡 Pearl River Ferry

090　第五章　港澳航线船型变迁

096　第六章　广东商船船型变迁大事记

105　下篇　广东航运文化 >

106　第一章　牵星术与海图

110　第二章　广东人"下南洋"

110　下南洋　To the Southeast Asia

113　下南洋的血泪史　The tragic history of Sailing to the Southeast Asia

116　广东人下南洋　Cantonese to the Southeast Asia

120　广东侨民对南洋的经济开发　Guangdong overseas Chinese for the Southeast Asian economic development

124　兰芳大统制共和国　Lan Fang Republic

126　第三章　"十三行"

126　广州十三行诞生　The born of Guangdong Shi San Hang

134　广州十三行辉煌史　The glorious history of Guangdong Shi San Hang

150　第四章　珠江游船文化

150　荔枝湾与艇仔粥　Litchi Bay and Sampan Congee

155　花艇与紫洞艇　Pleasure boat：Hua Boat and Zidong Boat

158　珠江夜游　Pearl River Night Cruise

163　第五章　轮船招商局在广东

164　轮船招商局成立　The establishment of China Merchants Steamship Navigation Company

171　轮船招商局在广东　China Merchant Steamship Navigation Company in Guangdong

上篇

海上丝绸之路与广东商船
The Maritime Silk Road and Guangdong Merchant Ship

"乾坤有序，宇宙无疆。星辰密布，斗柄指航。""富有冒险精神的人们，驾驶着当时属于世界最大型最先进的帆船，操作着本国发明的航海指南针，满载着早已闻名于世的中国陶瓷和丝绸同海外各国人民进行和平的商业往来，互通有无。"这描述的就是海上丝绸之路。海上丝绸之路是中国与世界其他地区进行经济文化交流的海上通道，是由东西洋间一系列港口网点组成的国际贸易网。

海上丝绸之路形成主因是中国南方沿海山多平原少且内部往来不易，地方诸侯也需海外资源交易以维持统治，东南沿海借助夏冬季风助航更增加了海陆的方便性，因此古代中国沿海很多地方有此项交流，可追溯至汉代或更早。唐中后期，陆上丝绸之路因战乱受阻加之同时期中国经济重心已转到南方，而海路又远比陆路运量大、成本低、安全度高，海路便取代陆路称为中外贸易热忱，使海上丝绸之路达到空前繁盛。明朝海禁，海上丝绸之路渐没落，郑和下西洋实质是朝廷性质的航海行为，难以为继，无法持久，海禁迫使民间海外贸易转型为走私性质的私商贸易。民间海外贸易的需求张力和朝廷政策的矛盾冲突始终贯穿明清两朝，无政治武装支持的中国海商无力挑战大航海后政治军事商业合一的西方扩张势力，海禁导致中国退出海洋竞争，是近代中国积弱落后的关键。

The Maritime Silk Road is the sea passage between China and the rest of the world in economic and cultural exchanges. It is an international trade network consisting of a series of port outlets between the east and the west.

Maritime Silk Road is formed mainly because that the southern Chinese coastal areas have lots of mountains but little valleys, which made the internal exchanges very hard. What's more, local princes also needed overseas trade to maintain the rule. The southeast coast with the aid of summer and winter monsoon has increased the convenience of land and sea transport, thus the ancient Chinese coastal areas had this exchange, that can be traced back to the Han Dynasty or earlier. In the late Tang Dynasty, the Silk Road on the land was hampered by the war, and the center of China's economy had shifted to the south. Compared with the land transport, sea transport had such a range of advantages as considerable capacity, low cost and high security. The sea road replaced the land transport and becomes more and more popular. Sea transport was banned in the Ming dynasty, which led to the decline of it. Zheng He's travel was an action of the government, which couldn't be continued. The sea ban forced the transformation of private overseas trade into smuggling private trade. The demand for private overseas trade tension and the contradictions and conflicts of the court policy has always run through the Ming and Qing dynasties, and China's maritime business, which has no political armed support, has failed to challenge the Western expansion forces of political and military commercial unity after navigating. The ban made China exit from maritime competition, which was the key to the backwardness of modern China.

第一章 古代海上丝绸之路与广东商船
The Maritime Silk Road and Guangdong Merchant Ship

广州是"海上丝绸之路"的发祥地和始发港,自秦汉时期以来,世界各国商船都沿着"广州通海夷道"到广州经商贸易,采购商货。

早在18世纪,瑞典东印度公司就曾经三次派商船"哥德堡"号(East Indiaman Gotheborg)远航至广州采购,最后沉没于瑞典近海。时光荏苒,岁月沉淀,见证了"海上丝绸之路"空前繁盛的"哥德堡Ⅰ"号和其满仓货物等待重见天日的时刻。1984年,瑞典一次民间考古活动发现了沉睡海底的"哥德堡Ⅰ"号残骸。

1993年,瑞典新东印度公司开始筹划仿造"哥德堡"号。2003年6月,经过十年的精心打造,这艘使用18世纪工艺制造的"哥德堡"号新船顺利下水。2005年10月2日清早,新"哥德堡"号重新验证"海上丝绸之路"的航线,由瑞典的哥德堡港起航,最后抵达广州。这次创举再次验证了"海上丝绸之路"由广东始发的史实。

提及海运,必不能不提造船业,造船业为航海贸易提供了运载的工具,自古如是。据史料考证,早在秦汉时期,广东已经出现了成熟的南船船型。到清朝末年民国初期时,广州已经成为中国南方造船业的集中所在地。1851年在黄埔长洲岛建成的柯拜船坞是中国最早建成的三大船坞之一。新中国成立至今,广州一直是中国三大造船基地之一,广州地区的船舶设计单位和船厂近20年来设计和建造的各类船舶,除国内使用之外,还遍布世界各地,受到国外客商的一致好评。

上篇 海上丝绸之路与广东商船

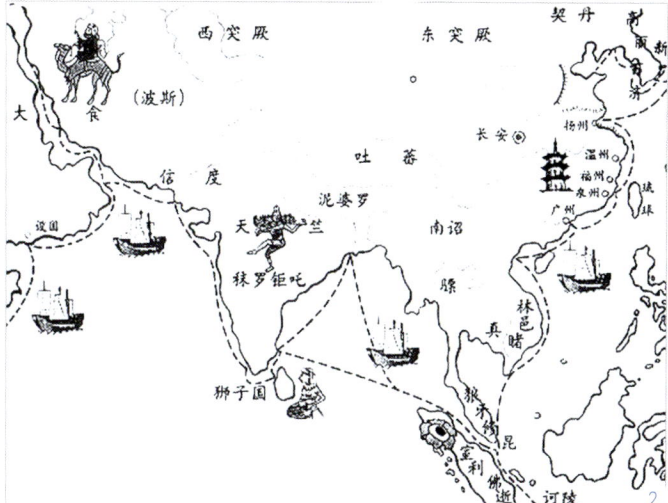

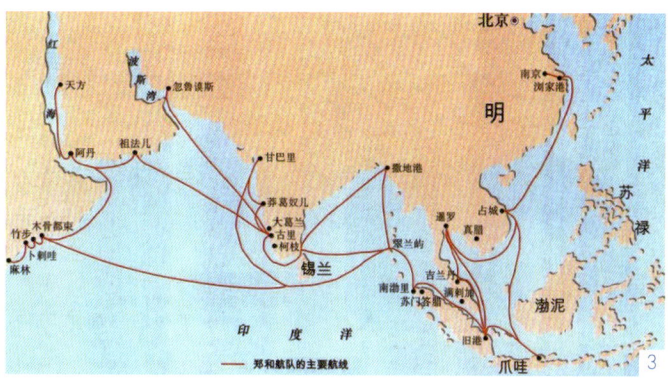

1. 西人所绘海上丝绸之路图
The western painting of Maritime Silk Road

2. 唐宋海上丝绸之路图
The Maritime Silk Road of Tang and Song dynasties

3. 郑和下西洋路线图
The map of Zheng He's voyages to the West

回顾古代的"海上丝绸之路",无论是广州还是泉州、宁波……出洋贸易,首先是把进行贸易的商品装船,船是载体,船的作用是依靠它的适航性能、安全性能、装载舱容,把大宗商品带到目的港进行贸易。

像《合浦与海上丝绸之路》所述"古代'海上丝绸之路'探索早于西周,民路成于战国,商路繁于秦朝,官路通于西汉……新石器晚期的史前壮举'越人大迁徙'迁移的过程中就开辟了我国东南亚各地的远洋航线……"。作为徐闻、合浦这两个最早被历史记述为起航点的"城镇",经考证距今一万年前,开始进入新石器时代。可以说岭南是个有历史的地方,只不过在秦汉之前是"陆梁地",没有文字记述,却是有文化的地方。《吕思勉读史札记·官南方者之贪》语:"贸易往来,水便于陆,故南琛之至尤早。《史记·货殖列传》言番禺为珠玑、犀、玳瑁、果、布之凑,此语必非言汉时,可见陆梁之地未开,蛮夷贾船,已有来至交广者矣。"这是史前的广东。

海上丝绸之路主要交通工具是船,岭南在秦之前就有船!新石器晚期的遗址珠海高栏岛宝镜湾岩画,有七条船图,是两头翘的船,这是4000年前的画。

珠海高栏岛宝镜湾岩画
Rock paintings of Zhuhai Island Gaolan Hokyo Bay

《广东船研究》述:"天才石"岩画有一个船的图形,船长85厘米,船头细长尖翘,头顶装饰似鸟头,船身以两条线构成,后部竖一长竿,竿高75厘米,竿上向后飘一旗幡之类的物体,有人认为是船桅和帆,船呈方形,船下刻有水波纹,另外有两个人和三个似船锚或弓弩的图形,均与胎不相连。"大坪石"岩画的中心内容围绕着一条大船,船头有'龙头'似的装饰,船高0.35米,长1.5米,船前聚集20多个人物和少量动物,大小不等,高在17厘米至35厘米之间。船停岸边,人在岸边绕着船欢庆,左前有二人沿跳板往船上爬,下面是集聚海岸边的人群,人群中可看出手舞足蹈的多种人物形象……内容应该是庆祝大船出海归来。"藏宝洞"东壁岩画以船为中心,……从右上部至左下边,有四只船在海中排列,大小不一,花纹不一,形状相似,均为两头尖,底近平。

清同治年间,乡人曾在虞州(即合浦)九头岭下发现船厂遗址,挖掘出造船木材,坚硬如铁,其中方形大木,长达20丈,可以想象当时船厂规模之大。这个遗址是战国时期的战船造船厂遗址。事实上司马迁也确实知道岭南在秦汉时期造船。他在《史记·上父偃列传》中曰:赵佗"将楼船之士南攻百越"。越人能造一种"戈船","戈船"也是一种可用于日常交通运输,又可用于军事行动的一种船只,《史记集解》引张晏语曰:"越人于水中负人船,又有蛟龙之害,故置戈于下,因以为名也。"戈船应该是边架艇,小船加上单架或双架,航行虽遇风浪,不易倾覆。架的形式似戈,或许也是戈船名称的由来。

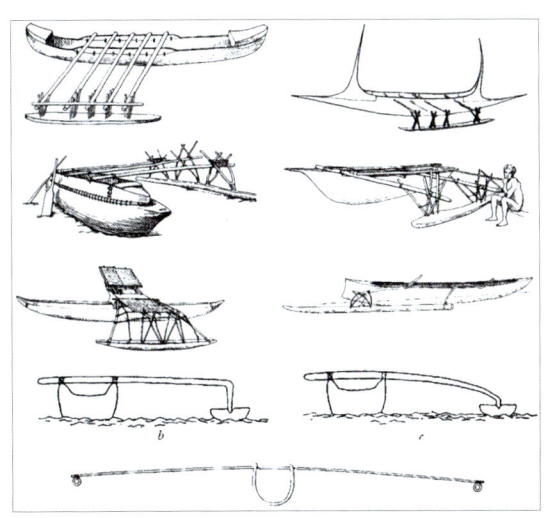

戈船(边架艇)
Ge ship (side frame boat)

汉武帝平南越后，中国由合浦、徐闻出发的商船所携带物品多为"黄金""杂缯"等往东南亚。它们沿海梯航，贸易之船回程所携带的货物则常是玻璃制品、水晶、玛瑙、犀角、象牙和香料等国内稀缺又珍奇之货。广州出土的东汉陶质货船模是实施梯航船舶的代表船型，该船的剖面型线如同客船，是一种小平底、两端微上翘的主体，其上层建筑比较复杂，但不会相似于明清所画的楼船那样高大。

1

2

1. 东汉陶质货船模
Ceramic cargo vessel model in the Eastern Han Dynasty

2. 东汉陶质客船模
Pottery craft in the Eastern Han Dynasty

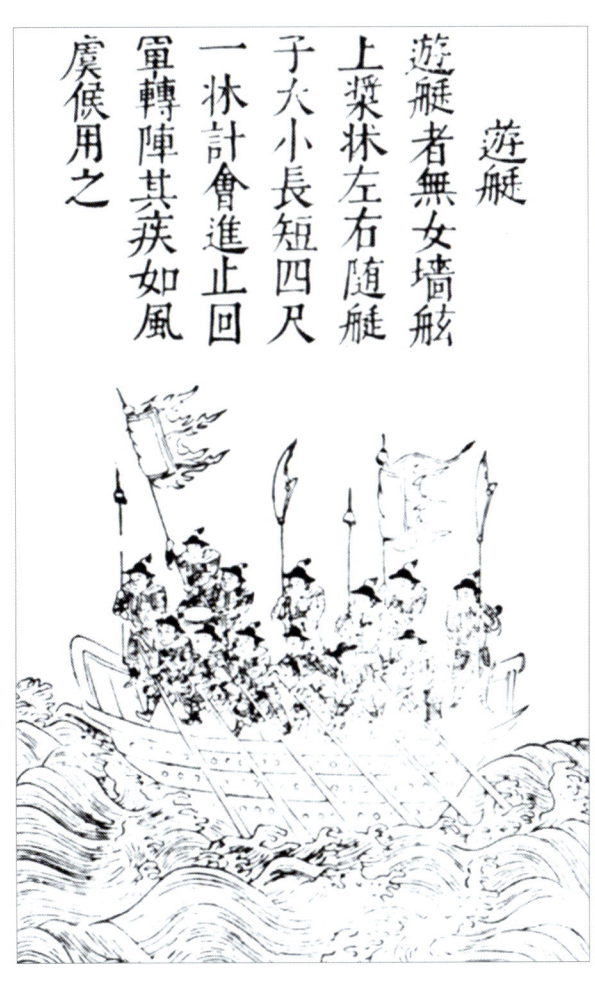

古代战舰之游艇木兰舟
Mulan, an ancient warship

隋唐以后，广东对外贸易迅速发展、膨胀，造船技术不断提高，船也不断适应远洋航海，且有了水密隔舱。唐代广东诞生了木兰舟，《岭南代答》卷六云："浮南海而南，舟如巨室，帆若垂天之云，柂长数丈，一舟数百人，不忧巨浪，而忧浅水也。"《新唐书》则曰：木兰舟是一种大海船，能载一千人。当时航行于南海、印度洋的巨舶在波斯湾航行只能止于阿拉伯河下游及今阿巴丹港一带，而因吃水太深不能西至幼发拉底河口。正如"舟如巨室，帆若垂天之云，柂长数丈"，及"一舟数百人，中积一年粮，豢豕酿酒其中"一说。

宋元是海外贸易的极盛时期，泉州逐渐加入南海航行，到南宋后期在一定程度上代替了广州的地位。南海、印度洋上的帆船穿梭，其中最常见的是中国帆船。1974年夏，在福建泉州湾的后渚港出土了一艘远洋海船航海货船，经复原该船船长30米，船宽10.5米，深5.0米，上宽下窄，尖底大侧舷，大约沉没在南宋景炎元年（1276年）前后，是目前世界上最古老的宋代三桅木帆海船，属于我国古代四大船型之一的福船型，载重量约200吨，相当于唐代一支700头骆驼的运输队驮运的重量。具有结构坚固、抗风抗浪力强、吃水深、稳定性好的特点。

后渚港宋船出土现场（1974年）
The site of the excavation of the HouZhu harbor boat (1974)

阳江南宋木质沉船"南海一号"（1987年）
South China No.1, the wooden wreck in Yangjiang in the Southern Song Dynasty

广东阳江海域打捞上来一艘南宋时代的木质沉船"南海一号"，它长30米、宽10多米、高3~4米，载重量八百多吨，堪称海上"巨无霸"。

明代虽然海外贸易因国情问题逐渐走下坡路，但明代是中国造船技术的顶峰时期，船型、风帆部是最先进的，郑和七下西洋的宝船队足以说明。关于明代的船型，在郑若曾《筹海阁编》、茅以仪《武备志》、沈启《南船记》里都有文字记述和丰富的图例。《武备志》曰："广船视福船尤大，其坚致亦远过之。盖广船乃铁力木所造，福船不过松杉之类而，二船在海，若相冲击，福船即碎，不能挡铁力之坚也。倭夷造船，亦用松杉之类，不敢与广船相冲，但广船难调，不如调福船为便易，广船若坏，须用铁力木修理，难乎其继，且其制上窄下宽，状若两翼，在里海则稳，在外洋则动摇。此广船之利弊也。广东大战胎用火器于浪漕中，起伏荡漾，未必能中贼，即使中矣，亦无几何，但可借此以褫敌人之心胆耳。"

蔚蓝船说——广东商船船型变迁

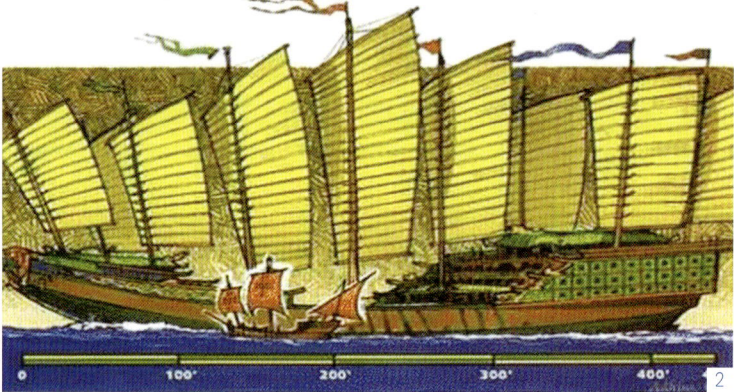

1. 16世纪中国明朝的宝船，船身巨大
Treasure ship in the Ming Dynasty in the Ming Dynasty

2. 郑和宝船和"哥伦布·圣玛丽亚"号的比例
The ratio of Zheng He's treasure ship to the Columbo Saint Maria

3. 明朝水师编队
The Navy Fleet

1. 珠海"金华兴"号
Jin Huaxing boat in Zhuhai

2. 红头船
Red head boat

　　清代虽是一口通商使广州有得天独厚之感，但一口通商并非意味着广州是独家经营，广船、福船、鸟船都可以航行于南海。从1971年澄海出土的红头船现场照片来看，当时红头船是尖底圆舭，而曾经航行于南海的菲律宾、印度尼西亚等地的"金华兴"号是尖头平底的海船。

　　人们历来把红头船当作清代潮州地区从事远洋贸易的商船，大多数潮籍华侨就是乘坐红头船到海外谋生，寻求发展。红头船曾经是中国同世界各地经济和文化交流的纽带，也是各地华侨同祖国联系的纽带。清朝雍正时代，南方海盗横行，广东潮州、惠州尤为严重。当时的政府没有足够的水师对付海盗，只好采用坚壁清野的做法，通过对民船编甲互保的控制，切断民船渔船与海盗的联系，以达到防范海盗的目的。规定各省商船渔船在船体两端头尾部位和大桅上半截用油漆涂上不同颜色，并刊刻某省某州县、某字某号等字，以便于进行审批、登记、发牌、稽查等船政管理。因广东在南，南方属火，用色为赤，赤即红色。应用"红油漆饰，青色钩字"（青，青丝之青，也就是指黑色）；而江苏在其他三省之北，北方属水，用色为黑，"青油漆饰，白色钩字"；浙江即为西方的白色，"白油漆饰，绿色钩字"；福建则为东方的绿色，"绿油漆饰，红色钩字"（俗称为"绿头船"）。四省的船以四色作为区别。而红头船还特意在船头画上像鸡眼的黑圈，认为船头画上眼睛，才不会迷失航道。

第二章 21世纪海上丝绸之路，广船再出发
21st-Century Maritime Silk Road, Guangdong ship sets out again

共同建设"21世纪海上丝绸之路"
Jointly build "21st-century Maritime Silk Road"

1949年新中国成立之后至1978年，这段特殊的时期，广州很难发挥出大港口的历史优势。1978年后，广州对外贸易进入一个新的发展时期，由于历史优势和渊源，广交会成为中国对外贸易招商的大舞台。随着航运业的大船化趋势对深水港的要求，广州港也由河港转为海港，主力港已由黄埔港移至珠江口几何中心的南沙深水港。

2013年10月，习近平主席出访东盟成员国印度尼西亚、马来西亚并出席APEC峰会。他在讲话中明确指出：东南亚地区自古以来就是"海上丝绸之路"的重要枢纽，中国愿同东盟国家加强海上合作，使用好中国政府设立的中国-东盟海上合作基金，发展好海洋合作伙伴关系，共同建设"21世纪海上丝绸之路"。国务院总理李克强在2014年3月5日所做的政府工作报告中提出"抓紧规划建设丝绸之路经济带和21世纪海上丝绸之路"。自此，"21世纪海上丝绸之路"成为国家发展战略。

"海上丝绸之路"一直是沟通东西方经济文化交流的重要桥梁，而东南亚地区自古就是海上丝绸之路的重要枢纽和组成部分。"21世纪海上丝绸之路"是我国在世界格局发生复杂变化的当前，主动创造合作、和平、和谐的对外合作环境的有力手段，为我国全面深化改革创造良好的机遇和外部环境。"21世纪海上丝绸之路"的战略合作伙伴并不仅限与东盟，而是以点带线，以线带面，增进同沿边国家和地区

的交往,将串起连通东盟、南亚、西亚、北非、欧洲等各大经济板块的市场链,发展面向南海、太平洋和印度洋的战略合作经济带,以亚欧非经济贸易一体化为发展的长期目标。由于东盟地处海上丝绸之路的十字路口和必经之地,将是新海丝战略的首要发展目标,而中国和东盟有着广泛的政治基础、坚实的经济基础,"21世纪海上丝绸之路"战略符合双方共同利益和共同要求。

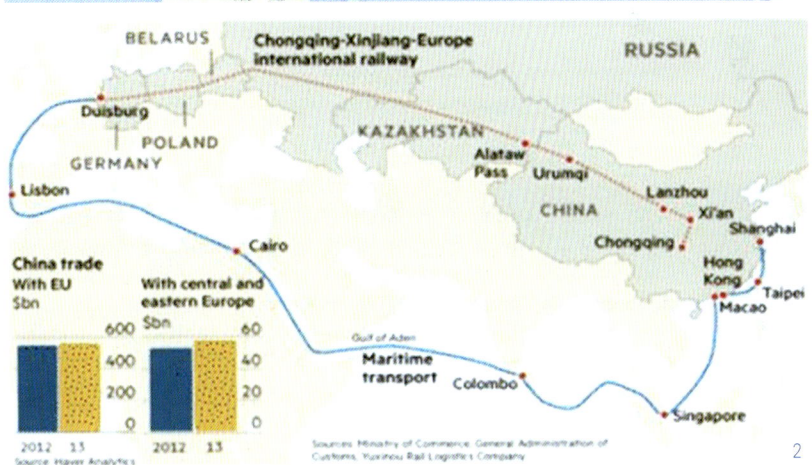

1. 海上丝绸之路与陆上丝绸之路
The Maritime Silk Road and Silk Road on the land

2. 21世纪海上丝绸之路
21st-Century Maritime Silk Road

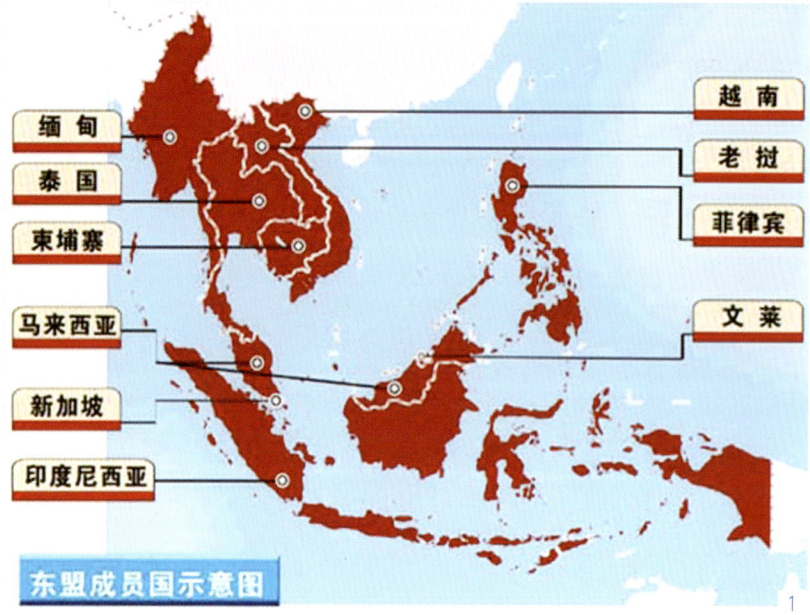

1. 东盟成员国
ASEAN members

2. 21世纪海上丝绸之路周边国家及地区
Neighboring countries and regions of 21st - century Maritime Silk Road

新世纪机遇
Opportunities in the new century

历史进入21世纪，中国人下南洋的脚步并没有停止，但原因和动机已经发生了很大的变化。可以预见，随着中国经济实力的进一步提升，"下南洋"的中国人还会越来越多。而随着中国—东盟自由贸易区建成及加紧推进，随着区域经济合作战略构想的实施，中国人的南洋之路，会越走越宽。

1. 中国—东盟自由贸易区建成庆祝仪式
To celebrate the establishment of Chinese - ASEAN Free Trade Area

2. 中国—东盟博览会
China - ASEAN Expo

中篇

图说广东商船船型变迁
The Change of Guangdong Merchant Ship

广东地处岭南，东、东南、南、西南三面临海，海岸线长达2500公里。省内河流纵横遍布全省，是国内典型的河网省份之一。主要河流有珠江、韩江、漠阳江、鉴江等，珠江为东江、西江、北江的总称，是省内最大的水系；粤东的韩江是第二大河。从上古时期开始，由于有海河水网，海河交通便利，使广东古代有发达的造船业与之相适应。但是，由于广东本土经济起步较迟，在秦统一岭南（公元前214年）之前广东还是一个没有国家、没有城镇、没有文字，被司马迁称之为"陆梁地"的蛮夷之地。这块土地没有为我们留下秦以前的历史记录，所以，我们对秦以前的广东知之甚少。

中篇　图说广东商船船型变迁

第一章　古代广东商船船型（1840年以前）
Guangdong merchant ship in ancient times (Before 1840)

古代中国是造船及航海大国，享有盛名。广东船舟自汉代起已有史料记载，唐代的广州通海夷道，明代的"广船"（古中国四大名船之一）更是闻名遐迩，航运发达和海贸繁荣。

甲骨文"舟"，是象形字，一只小船首尾窄中间宽，还有几个格档，非常形象。古文字的显示，说明在文字出现之前中国已经越过了独木舟时期，进入了木板船时代。

金文"造"是会意字，金文录自"毛公鼎"和"颂鼎"，这象征了西周前，我国造船是在室内发展起来的，在一个有上盖的屋子里建造，边上则是个舟字，这就是我们传统意义上的"闭门造舟"。到了许慎《说文解字》一书中篆文"造"字则把房拆了，说明也有了室外造船。

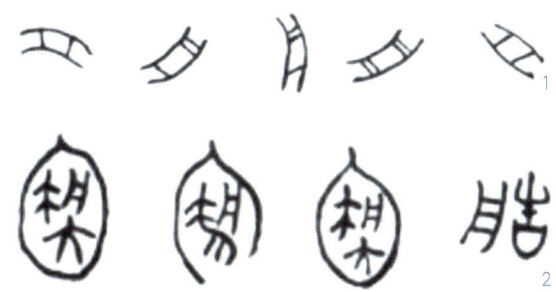

1. 甲骨文"舟"
Oracle "boat"

2. 金文"造"
Clementi "made"

广东最古老的船舶记载
Records of the oldest ships in Guangdong

据《广东通史》记载，商代末年及西周时期广东已有奴隶主和奴隶出现。春秋战国时代，奴隶制在广东部分发达地区获得一定的发展，到战国后期，这部分地区已经进入阶级社会。

而就是在这个时期，历史开始记载广东的造船。《吕氏春秋·慎大览》记载有"适越者坐，有舟也"，这就是说南方百越是善于造舟的，广东的南越先民，早在新石器时代便已经开始使用舟楫。虽然当时广东经济文化并不发达，但是因为海河水网密布，为了适应这样的自然环境，民间已经开始学会了制造舟楫，而当时的船应该是独木舟，再往后进化便有独木舟与独木舟用竹钉钉上几块木板组合成的早期"木板船"。因为是民间自造，因此这些木板船并未批量生产。

《珠海考古发现与研究·高栏岛宝镜湾石刻岩画与古遗址的发现与研究》一书为广东造船发展研究提供了极其重要的资料。

1989年发现的珠海高栏岛宝镜湾遗址是四千年前新石器时期的遗址，其天才

天才石岩画：岩画中有一艘船的图形，船长85厘米，船头细长尖翘，头顶装饰似鸟头，船身以两条线构成，后部竖一长竿，竿高75厘米，竿上向后飘一旗幡之类的物体，有人认为是船桅和帆，船呈方形，船下刻有水波纹

石、大坪石、藏宝洞三处岩画被认定为同时期的画，考古发现画里有七艘大小不同的船，只是渔船，这是广东最古老的船舶历史记载，对广东造船史来说是最精彩、最宝贵和前所未有的史料。

1. 藏宝洞岩画：整幅画以船桅中心，从右上到左下，有四艘船在海中排列，大小不一，花纹不一，形状相似，均为两头尖，底近平。右上方的船最为明显，船的两头尖翘，船边和船底平直，船身正中近船舷处刻饰两个相连的云雷纹，中部刻一条水波纹，靠近船头处的水波纹变成云雷纹，船的上面、中间为相对的卷云纹，两边有一些无法辨认的线纹，这些纹饰可能与行船的天气相关。右上方船的左下方为画的正中，有一大一小两只船，头尾相交错，小船在左上方，大船在右下方，大船的船头尖翘，头顶分三个尖，船体较深，船身刻三个云雷纹，形似三只眼睛的兽面纹，船下的花纹和生物难以辨认，船的上面有四个人，三人手上举，腿分立，一个侧身蹲立，人手的上面举一个平台，小船两头尖，船身刻鱼鳞形花纹。船上为一形象生动逼真的猴子，左下部有一大船，大船船身较长，船头尖翘，尖头向上伸出两角，角顶分枝相连，呈倒三角形，船身有曲折形装饰花纹，船尾上翘，平顶上有一圆头，船中站立一人，船之前有一动物图像

2. 大坪石岩画：岩画的中心内容围绕着一条大船，船头有"龙头"形装饰，船高0.35米，长1.5米，船前聚集20多个人和少量动物，人和动物大小不等，高在17厘米至35厘米之间。船停靠在岸边，人在岸边朝着船欢庆，船的左前方有二人沿着跳板往船上爬，下面是集聚海岸边的人群，人群手舞足蹈，庆祝海船归来

独木舟
The canoe

独木舟,顾名思义是由一条木制成的舟船,古语曰:"刳木为舟,剡木为楫",独木舟是刳制而成的。最早刳制独木舟的工具是石器,用锋利的石器刳制烧烤过的大圆木制成独木舟是古代先民创造的加工工艺。

1983年9月,在化州中垌长湾河牛牯坡河段冲出两艘独木舟,据化州文化局提供

1. 刳制独木舟
Canoe

2. 广东汉代化州独木舟
Huazhou canoe of Guangdong in the Han Dynasty

的资料描述，在两艘独木舟出土的同时，还有红椎、白椎、水翁等地下古墓出土。

化州出土独木舟
Huazhou canoe of Guangdong in the Han Dynasty

古战船——南越王船
Ancient warship - Nanyue Boat

西汉南越王陵墓出土的船纹提筒，显示了四艘环形船纹，造型美观。该船一艘由独木舟向木板船进化的过渡船只，是海船。就是说它们是"广船"的祖先，在不迟于新石器晚期，广东已有了可以在南海航行的海船。

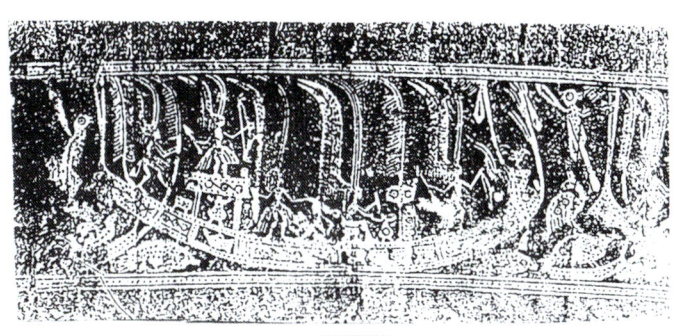

南越王船（线描图由吕烈民制作）
The Nan Yue Boat
(line drawings produced by Lv Liemin)

西汉木板船
Wooden ship in the Western Han Dynasty

广州西村皇帝岗出土的木板船模,整船造型美观、完整,是一艘划桨的客船模型。其船型与"南越王船"相比较,显示了战船向民船发展的变化,船体已有了型线,首尾宽度比中间小,这与甲骨文"舟"极其相似(足见文字是实体的象形),并有了封闭的"楼"和尾"舵"手(以桨代舵,掌握航向)。

西汉木板船模(复制件)
The Western Han Dynasty wooden ship model (copy)

东汉陶船模
Pottery ship in the Eastern Han Dynasty

广州水荫路出土东汉陶船模(客船),这是一艘船体体型很先进的船只,其中船尾的桨舵,船头悬挂的碇(锚)是目前发现的世界上最早的舵和锚。该船模显示了广东造船发展之神速,从西汉到东汉船舶的舾装齐全,处于世界领先水平。

广州红花岗出土的东汉陶制模(货船)。其结构形制较简,船体稍短而宽,首尾狭,中部较宽,底平。船上横架"梁担"八根,"梁担"之上有立柱以置篙。是以篙推进的内河货船,该船模中段肥胖,这种货船的设计完全符合现代科学。

1. 东汉陶船模（客船复制件）
Pottery ship (Passenger ship, copy) the Eastern Han Dynasty

2. 东汉陶船模（货船）
Pottery ship (Cargo ship) the Eastern Han Dynasty

八槽舰

Eight boat ship

东晋末年徐道覆、卢循义军占领广州后建造了九艘八槽舰，所谓八槽即是将船体分成八个水密舱，为船舶的安全航行提供保证，水密隔舱技术是中国在长期航海实践中的一项伟大发明，是对世界造船与航海的重大贡献之一。现代的船舶一舱不沉的概念即来自于"八槽舰"，可见其影响之深远。

八槽舰（复原船模）
Eight boat ship (recovery ship model)

唐代战船与民船
The warship and privateers in the Tang Dynasty

我国造船技术的提高与应用始于唐代，尤其表现在战船上。唐张九皋、杜佑在广州任职期间建行过六种战船：楼船、艨艟、斗舰、走舸、游艇、海鹘。楼船之名最早始于战国时期南方的越国，越有楼船军，秦朝及汉朝都有官衔为"楼船将军"的军事指挥官。当年开凿灵渠，南下岭南的就是楼船。汉武帝平南越，水路攻入番禺的就是楼船。其船高首宽，外观似楼，船大楼高，在古代很大程度上担任了水战主力舰船。但由于船只过高，重心不稳，故多在内河水战中担任主力。

而随着对外贸易的不断发展与扩大，唐代的海上运输船舶体积有所增大，体型增肥，向大圆弧发展。唐代的著名海船有木兰舟、苍柏等。木兰舟是用木兰木建造，是一种大海船，能载一千人，《岭南代答·卷六》中说："浮南海而南，舟如巨室，帆若垂天之云，柂长数丈，一舟数百人，中积一年粮，豢豕酿酒其中，置死生于度外。……又大食国更越西海，至木兰皮国，则其舟又加大矣。一舟容千人，舟上有机杼市井，或不遇便风，则数年而后达，非甚巨舟，不可至也。"

1. 楼船（复原船模）
Lou boat (recovery ship model)

2. 木兰舟（复原船模）
Mu Lan boat

宋元大航海时代
Navigation Era in the Song and Yuan Dynasties

宋朝在造船业和航海业上取得巨大的进步，开始取代穆斯林在东亚和东南亚的海上优势。元朝后中国的船只体积最大，装备最佳，拥有世界上最庞大的帆船舰队和商船队，以及最好的造船业和航海技术，大型海船的载重达到了500～600吨，同时还能搭乘500～600人，"远洋巨型海船，船底和两舷用两层或三层木板，有四层舱室，共有房间50～100间左右，一般4～6桅，每船8～10橹，每橹4人。甚至有一船20橹的。"中国在世界经济中也居主导地位，从东北亚的日本、高丽，到东南亚各地和印度沿海，乃至波斯湾和东非各港口，已经形成一个活跃的贸易网络。中国的商人往来海上，蔚蓝的海面上常年行驶着庞大的中国远洋船队；回首内陆，是庞大的丝绸、瓷器、茶叶供应基地，这些深受国外客商欢迎的产品，汇聚到海岸线上的各个港口，然后再装上随着季风而来的船只……一条海上丝绸之路，连通了中国和世界，把陶瓷、丝绸运往世界各地，也把灿烂的中华文明运往世界各地。

宋元广东海船向大型发展，这些远航南海各国的大海船均为民间制造，不但数量多，而且质量高，比以前具有更多特色：船体更巍峨高大，结构更坚固合理，行船工具更趋完善，装修更为华美，其船头小，尖底呈V字形，便于破浪前进；身扁宽，体高大、吃水深，受到横向狂风袭击仍很稳定；结构坚固，穿上多樯多帆，便于使用多面风；大船中也有探水设备。特别是开始使用指南针进行导航，开辟了航海史的新时期。

广东阳江海域打捞上来一艘南宋时期的木质沉船"南海一号"，它长30米、宽10多米、高3～4米，载重量800多吨，堪称海上"巨无霸"。"南海一号"是迄今为止世界上已发现的海上沉船中年代最早、船体最大、保存最完整的的远洋贸易商船，文物及考古价值足以与秦朝兵马俑、敦煌石窟和北京故宫媲美。

1. "南海一号"（复原船模）
Nan Hai No.1(recovery ship model)

2. 元海船
Ships of the Yuan Dynasty

3. 南宋车船
Transportation in the Southern Song Dynasty

明清大海船与大航海时代同时到来
The advent of large ships and navigation era in the Ming and Qing Dynasties

明永乐三年六月十五日（1405年7月11日）（600年后的这一天——2005年7月11日，我国有了自己首个"航海日"），大明帝国仰仗着强大的国力，派遣郑和统率拥有200多艘海船、2.7万多人的当时世界上最大规模的船队首航南中国海和印度洋，大海船与大航海时代同时到来。"云帆高张，昼夜星驰"，遍及亚非30多个国家和地区。这个壮举比哥伦布发现美洲新大陆早87年，比达伽马绕过好望角早98年，比麦哲伦到达菲律宾早116年，这是是明朝强盛的直接体现。

这一时期中国著名的船种分广船、福船、沙船和鸟船等四种。其中，广船、福船最为重要，它们都属于尖圆底船型，适航海阔水深多岛礁的区域，其共同点是吃水较深的圆、尖船底，艏部尖削，利于破浪；中部设置强大的纵向外置肋骨，坚固船身，可承受巨大风浪冲击；船舱内侧设置横肋和隔舱板组成的基本骨架，与龙骨形成纵横结构；多重船壳板，外壳板两侧舭部都设置不同形态的纵向附材或台阶式凸起，以抗击远洋航行中风浪引起的横向摇摆。

"广船"之名源于明代，专指广东建造的船舶。广船的结构坚实，闻名中外，有"广船代表中国造船史上最高水平"一说，它有水密隔舱、开孔舵、转轴舵、大扇形硬帆等世界先进技术，航行性能优秀。明代的战船与民船没有严格的区分，民间的优秀船只就是战船。所不同的是加装了作战设施。明代战将对广船的评价很高，其原因就是广船的船型优秀，选用高端的建造材料，适合于海上航行和水上作战。广东船、新会尖尾船、东莞大头船都是明代著名的战船。其造船讲究材料、建造工艺和质量，在结构要求坚实、耐用处常使用铁力木、乌婪木（乌木），或其他硬木，甚至底板也用铁力木，铁力木的强度是杉木的3倍，坚实的船舶强度，使广船被称为"广船铁力木为之"，作为战船它能犁沉、撞沉倭船，因此负有盛名，也因之成为我国四大名著古船种之一。

自唐"广州通海夷道"畅通后，南海的航行摆脱了梯航，往东南亚、去印度洋可以直航。南海的滔天海浪对航行的船舶提出了更高的要求，广船的主要航区就在南海，它的发展与南海海域、南海的海况练习更加紧密。明代广东有名的民用货船有乌艚、大头船及横江船，都是远洋海船。乌艚船一直使用到清代作为红头船的一种航行南海、东南亚等地。"其飘洋者曰白艚、乌艚，合铁力木为之，形如槽然，故曰艚。首尾又状海鳅（鲸），白者有两黑眼，乌者有两白眼。海鳅远见以为同类，不吞噬。"广东船分别在广州、潮州、琼州、高州设厂建造。

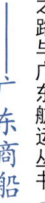

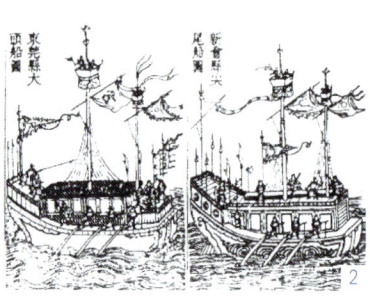

1. 大型广船（复原船模）
Large shipyard (recovery ship model)

2. 广东著名的战船：广东船、东莞大头船、新会尖尾船
Famous warships in Guangdong : Guangdong ship, Dongguan ship, and Xinhui Rat-tail ship

3. 乌艚船（白艚）
The boat ship (Bai Cao)

4. 乌艚船（乌艚）
The boat ship (Wu Cao)

福船

福船亦称"大福船",是一种尖底海船,以行驶于南洋和远海著称,明代我国水师以福船为主要战船。福船吃水四米,高大如楼,尖底上阔,首尾高昂,两侧有护板,全船分四层,下层装土石压舱,二层住兵士,三层是主要操作场所,上层是作战场所,居高临下,弓箭火炮向下发,往往能克敌制胜。其首部高昂,又有坚强的冲击装置,乘风下压能犁沉敌船,多用船力取胜。郑和下西洋船队的主要船舶叫宝船,它采用的就是中国古代适用于远洋航行的优秀船型——福船型。福船特有的双舵设计,在浅海和深海都能进退自如,载人和载货量均是一流,百叶窗一样的木质船帆可以使用多年不换,前进速度慢而稳,通常用来运载瓷器等易碎物品。

大型福船(复制船模)
Large Fu ship (recovery ship model)

沙船

沙船也叫作"防沙平底船",因其适于在我国北方海区水浅、多沙滩的航道上航行,故称沙船。在内河运输上具有运输量大、能适应河岸浅滩靠岸的特点。但在远洋海航方面体现出很大的弱点,元朝时,政府从长江流域调集900多艘沙船组成的舰队攻打日本,在日本西部的海域遇台风后几乎全军覆没,日本人称呼台风为"神风",即出自于此。所以一般用于内河运输和在远洋航行中在特殊季节作运输补给船使用。明茅元仪《武备志·军资乘·沙船》:"沙船能调戗使斗风,然惟便于北洋,而不便于南洋,北洋浅南洋深也。沙船底平,不能破深水之大浪也。北洋有滚涂浪,福船、苍山船底尖,最畏此浪,沙船却不畏此。"

1. 沙船(复原船模)
Lange junk(recovery ship model)

2. 鸟船(绿眉毛)
Bird ship (Lv Meimao)

鸟船

鸟船又称绿眉毛，是浙江沿海一带的海船，其特点是船首形似鸟嘴，故称鸟船。古代浙江人认为是鸟衔来稻谷种子，才造就了浙江的鱼米之乡，所以把船头做成鸟嘴状，由于鸟船船头眼上方有条绿色眉，故它又得名绿眉毛。在郑和船队中就有鸟船这种古船型。近年来，浙江新造一艘鸟船"绿眉毛"号，船长31米，宽6.8米，吃水深2.2米，排水量230吨；采用古老的木制舵，舵长31米，宽2.3米；有三桅五帆，其中主桅高24.5米，主帆三面，使用风力航速最高可达每小时9海里。

清代是广东商船最辉煌时代
Qing Dynasty: the most brilliant time of Guangdong merchant ships

清代是广船的顶峰期，清廷的一口通商政策不仅繁荣了广州的市场，同时也促进了广东的造船业。在明代"广船"的基础上，清代广船基本船型是首尖、上宽下窄、首低尾高，有尾艄、首脊弧小、首舷两侧油红色的三桅或二桅的"红头船"，主要用于海外贸易，据史记述为保证外贸的需要清代有海贸船1600艘，广州也因此成了清政府的"南库"（清政府的北库是山西的平遥）。其他还有艚船、包帆船、七艕船、米艇等，由于与外国船舶接触，在造船技术上产生互补，广船吸收了国外船舶技术改进了自身，广船进入最辉煌的年代。清代还保存着很大数量的战船，但因海禁，即使是战船也都限于双桅，主要对付百姓，但到清末期用来对付外来船只就船单力薄了。

红头船
Red head boat

大头艋

大头艋，亦称红单船（广东商人造船需禀报海关，给予红单以备稽查，故所造船名为"红头船"），产于顺德陈村，是道光咸丰年间南海上的头号大帆船，该船设计科学、合理，经济实惠。据史称其分载重为三十万司斤（约180吨）和五十万司斤（约300吨）两种。较大的船长10丈，载重50万司斤，船体大、坚实，行驶快速，每艘可安炮二三十门，船底部为鸡胸形、首部翘，尾部稍低于首。

七艕渔船

七艕渔船，是粤西地区常见的船型，拖网船。源于清中晚期，解放初期仍建造过，所以它也算是一种长寿船舶。中山、阳江、电白一带是七艕的诞生和发展地。大七艕船长66尺、宽13尺、深4.8尺，3桅；小七艕长60尺、宽11.6尺、深4.6尺，2~3桅。七艕以七道底板得名，船体狭长、底平，结构坚固，船头尖成劈型，易破浪，帆面积大、速度快、稳性好。

赶缯船

赶缯船，形制同红头船，可作战船、捕鱼和运送木材之用。

快蟹船

快蟹船，船两侧有成排的桨橹，外形活似蜈蚣和螃蟹，船体通常漆成红黑两色，元明时期叫"蜈蚣船"，清代称"快蟹"，出没于珠江口外贸的黄金水道，抢掠过往船只财务。原为走私船，由于其航行性能好，官府用于作缉私船。

Modelo de T'AU-MANG que figurou na Exposição de Paris de 1900

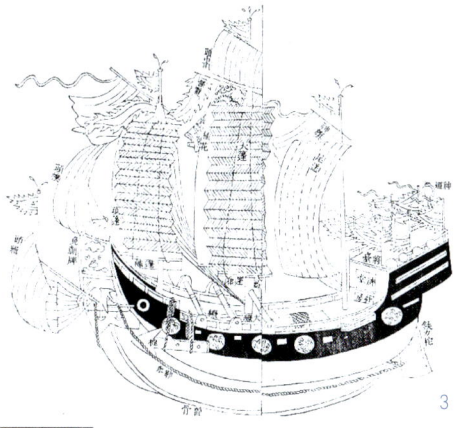

1. 头艋（Tan-Mang）模型
Tan-Mang model

2. 七艕渔船
Qi Bang fishing boat

3. 赶缯船
Warship: Gan Zeng boat

4. 快蟹船
Fast crab boat

人字桅帆船

人字桅帆船，多为客货船，海河兼用。

水师船

水师船，清政府的官船。广东省濒临南海，为了缉捕走私、海盗，很早就开始使用近代军舰，但由于不受朝廷重视，"南北洋有各省关协拨经费，或百余万，或数十万，用能宽裕经营，船械具备，而粤省则无之"，经费短缺，广东水师的舰船有一个很显著的特点，即多、小、乱，舰艇数量虽多，但吨位很小，只能用于内河和近海作战。

1. 人字桅帆船
Flip ship

2. 水师船（官船）
The navy ship

"中国皇后"号
The Empress of China

"中国皇后"号

  清乾隆四十九年二月二十二（1784年），"中国皇后"号离开了纽约港，满载着人参、皮革、贸易、胡椒、棉花以及铅等商品，驶往中国。这一年的8月下旬，"中国皇后"号终于到了当时作为中国海上门户之一的澳门，在这里取得了一章盖有清廷官印的"中国通行证"，获准进入珠江。在一名中国引水员的带领下，经过一天的航行，抵达广州的黄埔港。进港时，"中国皇后"号鸣礼炮十三响（代表当时美国的十三个州），其他停泊于缸内的各国商船也鸣炮回礼。格林船长曾有一则这样的手记："'中国皇后'号荣幸地升起了在这地域从未有人升起或看见过的第一面美国国旗！这一天是1784年8月28日。"

On February 22, 1784 (Qing Qianlong forty-nine years), 'Empress of China', left the port of New York, laden with ginseng, leather, sweater, pepper, cotton, lead and other goods, to China. In a Chinese pilot led, after a day of sailing, arrived in Guangzhou Whampoa port. When we were in port, 'Empress of China', a salute of Thirteen guns (representing Thirteen states USA at that time), the other at the harbor national merchant fired in reply. Captain Green has such a note 'Empress of China', to rise in this region has never been raised or seen the first USA flag! This day is August 28, 1784.

1. 英国东印度公司船队，1782年
British East India Company ships, 1782

2. 寄碇于黄埔港的美国商船亨利马克号
The moorings in the port of Whampoa America merchant Henry Mark

瑞典东印度公司的哥德堡号先后三次远航广州，第一次是1739年1月—1740年6月，第二次是在1741年2月—1742年7月，最有名的是第三次，在1743年3月—1745年9月。2006年7月18日上午，重建仿古商船哥德堡号胜利抵达广州港，受到中国人民的热烈欢迎。

Swedish East Indian company's Goteborg had three voyages in Guangzhou. The first time was from January 1739 to June 1740, and the second is from February 1741 to July 1742. The most famous is the third time, from the March 1743 to September 1745. On the morning of July 18, 2006, the reconstruction of the antique merchant ship Goteborg successfully arrived at Guangzhou Port, which was warmly welcomed by the Chinese people.

1. 瑞典"哥德堡"号帆船，1745年，广州
Sweden Goteborg sailboat in Guangzhou, 1745

2. 瑞典仿古商船"哥德堡"号，2006年，广州
The antique Swedish merchant ship Goteborg in Guangzhou, 2006

第二章 近代商船运输船型（1840—1949年）
Modern merchant ship (1840-1949)

　　清王朝道光二十年（1840年）鸦片战争爆发后，列强对中国开始了瓜分和掠夺，随着外国资本主义蜂拥侵入，封建制度开始解体，中国逐步沦为半封建半殖民地的国家。清政府被迫签订一系列不平等条约，香港被英帝国主义侵占，九龙被租借，新界被蚕食。随着中国门户的打开，珠江流域的广州、三水、江门、梧州、龙州、南宁等地相继被迫开放为对外通商口岸；被迫开放西江及珠江三角洲内河航运。继葡萄牙、西班牙之后，英、法、德、美等欧美资本主义国家的商船，相继涌入珠江水域，控制珠江航运，争夺珠江流域市场。广东的海运业被迫转入沿海与内河并逐步转向内河，原航行于省外与沿海的船舶，如：红头船、红单船（头艋）等已无用武之地，而步入改行和被淘汰的境地。至咸丰四年（1854年），抵达广州的外国商船有18个国家、300艘船舶，共15万多吨。其中英国船舶约占一半，独占进出口总额的三分之二。广州至香港航线的运输，几乎为洋商洋船所控制。由此，香港的航运业得到迅速发展，成为海洋与珠江航运的主要转运港，而广州在海上运输的地位却日益下降。

The Qing Dynasty Daoguang twenty years (1840) after the outbreak of the Opium War, imperialist powers began to divide and plunder China, with foreign capitalism poured into, the feudal system began to disintegrate, Chinese gradually reduced to a semi feudal and semi colonial country. The Qing government was forced to sign a series of unequal treaties, Hong Kong was occupied by the British imperialists, Kowloon on loan has been eroded, new territories. With the China portal was opened, the Pearl River Basin of

Guangzhou, Sanshui, Jiangmen, Wuzhou, Longzhou, Nanning and other places have been forced to open to foreign ports; to open the West River and Pearl River Delta inland shipping. In Portugal, Spain, Britain, Germany, France, and the United States, and other capitalist countries in Europe and American merchant, pouring into the Pearl River basin. Guangdong's overseas trade routes gradually alienated, which is one of the reasons behind the ship technology, Guangdong shipping industry was forced into coastal and inland river ships, and gradually turned to the original, sailing in the provinces and coastal areas such as : red head boat, single ship (red head has been watching) useless, and into and be diverted out of the situation. To Xianfeng four years (1854), the foreign merchant ships arrived in Guangzhou in 18 countries 300 ships for a total of more than 15 tons. The British ship accounts for about half of the ships in total, and two thirds of the total import and export trade. Guangzhou to Hongkong route of transportation, is almost controlled by taking ocean ship. Thus, the Hongkong shipping industry has developed rapidly and become the main port of transshipment of ocean and Pearl River shipping. Guangzhou is declining in its maritime transport status.

第一艘到达欧美的中国木帆船

Chinese Wooden masted boat: the first ship arrived in Europe and the United States

"耆英"号,是广船的骄傲,是中国唯一的一艘穿越好望角经纽约到达伦敦的全风力航行海船。远洋大帆船"耆英"号船长48.9米,宽10米,深4.8米,3桅纵帆,主桅杆高27米,重9吨;首桅高23米,尾桅高15米,悬挂式尾舵(开孔舵),载重800吨。

"耆英"号建成于清道光二十六年(1846年),其名称来自驻广州钦差大臣耆英。耆英因与英国签订了第一个不平等条约——《南京条约》,将香港割让给英国,在中国近代史上臭名昭著,可是"耆英"号帆船却声名远扬。该船在伦敦停靠时,英国维多利亚女皇等各方人士,都上船参观这第一艘到达欧美的中国木帆船。

"耆英"号堪称中国历代古船设计思想和建造技术的结晶,是中国古船宝库中的一件稀世珍品。

"耆英"号(1846年)
Qi Ying (1846)

1. "耆英"号（1847年，伦敦）
Qi Ying in London, 1847

2. "耆英"号船尾和船舵
Qi Ying stern and rudder

中国最后一艘三桅古帆船
The last Chinese ancient sailing ship

几乎在与耆英号建造的同时期,广东还建造了一艘"金华兴"号。"金华兴"号从外观上看,无论是船型、帆、舵、尾艄、结构用料等都是清末"广船"的典型,其船长24.6米,宽7米,主桅高21.5米,排水量800吨。船体宽大,船艏尖而低,船艉圆满而高翘,三桅,折角扇形帆。这艘广式古帆船是100多年前,由广东一带的造船厂制造的,尽管经历了一百多年风雨,但还完好无损,船底模板厚达8厘米,船底木材全部采用樟木,防火及防潮,而桅杆等选材于百年杉木,船只全部采用"入榫"方法建造,整条船未见有一只钉子,具有广式古帆船的典型特征。1986年落籍福建云霄县列屿镇,成为家族的捕鱼工具。"金华兴"号是整个中国海岸线最后一艘保存下来的三桅古式帆船,也是迄今发现的造型最大,保存最为完整的木质古帆船,极具文物保护价值。

"金华兴"号(2012年,珠海)
Jin Huaxing in Zhuhai, 2012

广东民俗——广东花尾渡
Guangdong folk - Hua Wei ferry

由于受外国船舶的影响，清末建造的船舶已经引进国外船舶的结构，使用先进的属具，并建造"小火"轮（一种机动客船）、拖轮等，开始安装蒸汽机推进。在内河"小火"轮开始了运作，内河的货运、客运则得到加速发展，珠江下游民用小火轮船拖带渡船逐渐增加，较大型的车渡也有用小火轮拖带。光绪三十四年（1908年），船商谭礼庭将大型车渡进行改装，拆去脚踏明轮装置，采用浅水船的平底，并仿照客货轮船的模式在船上建造餐厅，船头货仓改变不大，又吸取画舫的形式，在渡船的表面涂上绚丽夺目的彩画，看上去很像彩凤，遂被人称为"凤尾渡"。清末民初，航商又将凤尾渡的楼厅向前延伸，约占船身的五分之四，船分三层半。底舱装载货物；二层大舱桄客货舱，或加固，船头彩绘一只貔貅用以压邪，船尾两舷绘有花花绿绿的彩色图案装饰，远看色彩斑斓，渡船内部客舱两侧设有双层卧铺，并有华贵厢房、餐厅，又有浴室、卫生间设施，船上不设主机，由拖轮拖带航行，不受噪音之苦，使旅客感到方便舒适，是具有广东特色的一种独特船型——由车渡船发展为拍拖、吊拖的客货运船舶花尾渡，独具岭南特色。

脚踏渡船（图中可见尾部有六人正在出力踩水轮），林则徐曾于鸦片战争之初在广州制造过一艘脚踏明轮船，据史述，该脚踏车渡船是花尾渡的前身。1841年还造了一艘两头制柁，中设两轮以激水左右设桨36枝的水轮船

A foot Ferry (visible tail in six are output on turbine), Lin Zexu at the beginning of the Opium War in Guangzhou made a paddle steamers, according to the history of the bicycle, the ferry is the predecessor of tail crossing. In 1841 he built a boat for two pillars, arranged in two to 36 branches located around the propeller induced water water ship

蔚蓝船说 —— 广东商船船型变迁

21世纪海上丝绸之路与广东航运丛书 二

1. 20世纪70年代靠泊在广州珠江长堤的花尾渡
Hua Wei ferry that parked along the Pearl River in 1970s

2. 紫洞船，与花尾渡极其相似，是一种最豪华的游艇，舵在广福河面，无帆，船上宽敞舒适，陈设豪华。后来的花尾渡其外形就是仿造紫洞艇
Zi Dong ship is very similar with the tail crossing, and it is one of the most luxury yacht with gorgeous furnishings. The later tail crossing is a reproduction

花尾渡始于清末，其一直使用到20世纪七八十年代，最大的一艘即"曙光401"，20世纪20年代末，花尾渡已成为珠江下游的主要水上客运工具。抗战胜利后是花尾渡的鼎盛时期，以广州为中心，大小花尾渡航行于梧州、肇庆、江门、三埠、石歧5大航线。花尾渡是由机动拖轮拖带的优质木船，比较平稳，载客较多，大的船可载客三四百人，稍小的也可载一两百人，还可载几十吨货物。同时，花尾渡船体雄伟，装潢非常漂亮，穿行在珠江三角洲弯弯曲曲的河道上，犹如一座活动的水上宫殿，为华南独有的一景。

画舫也是一种高级娱乐船，早在一口通商时期在珠江上就大行其道
Restaurant is a senior pleasure boat and popular in the Pearl river in a trading period

第一艘来自欧洲的汽轮船
The first steam ship from Europe

"复仇女神"号为英国东印度公司于1835—1840年在利物浦建造的一艘远洋汽轮兵舰,是英国第一艘铁壳(用钢皮作外壳包装木船)及第一艘应用水密舱壁的军舰,同时也是世界海军史上最早使用蒸汽动力的军舰之一。该舰于1839年下水,吃水深度1.8米,排水量660吨,马力10匹,双引擎,铁质明轮推进,配备2门32磅及4门6磅大炮以及火箭弹,并可载船员90人,其动力来源除了水蒸汽轮外还有风帆。它是第一艘来自欧洲的汽轮船。

复仇女神号(1840年,广州)
Nemesis (Guangzhou, 1840)

我国第一艘蒸汽机轮船
China's first steam engine ship

"黄鹄"号蒸汽轮船是我国自行设计建造的第一艘蒸汽机明轮船,造价白银八千两。1865年在安庆内军械所由徐寿、华蘅芳设计建造的——"黄鹄"号船长17米,自重25吨;机舱设在前部,蒸汽机为单缸,缸长二尺,缸径一尺。该船试航于扬子江,在不到14个小时内逆流行驶了225公里,时速约28里。当曾国藩长子曾纪泽去北方省父时,这艘轮船将他的坐船托至高邮,他对轮船的性能甚为满意,遂将轮船命名为"黄鹄"号。"黄鹄"号是中国人自行研制,并以手工劳动为主建造成功的中国第一艘机动轮船,它的建造揭开了中国近代船舶工业发展的帷幕。

"江波"号是第一艘由国内民营工厂生产的蒸汽机拖轮,首航1876年,是陈子卿及其在清光绪二年(1876年)创办的西关新联泰机器厂制造的第一艘轮船。

　　在半封建半殖民地的中国,内河航运权被外国轮船公司操纵,不少外国轮船在珠江水面行驶。这些轮船有时机件发生故障,需要就地修理,便利用新联泰机器厂的场地和机器设备,由轮船派出随船技师、工匠指导该厂工人进行修理。因此,新联泰机器厂的工人便从实践中学会了一些修理轮船技术。陈澹浦看到当时珠江航运事业正在发展,制造轮船有发展前途,本厂工人又已掌握了一定的修理轮船技术,便派出他的孙子陈子卿,到福建马尾船厂和香港的船坞学习、考察造船技术,以便开展制造轮船业务。

　　1882年,陈子卿学成回厂,担任造船技师,在厂内设立设计部,设计制造轮船;又建立南栈、东栈两个工场,南栈在河南洗涌,专铸造大型部件——锅炉,东栈在天字码头江边,为装配轮船下水之所。经过近两年的努力,第一艘由广州民办工厂新联泰机器厂制造的,以蒸汽机为动力的轮船终于成功诞生,命名为"江波"号。由于船身较轻,适合在内河行驶,租金又比外国的轮船便宜,不少航商都乐意租用。陈子卿乘时扩展业务,连续制造了江汉、江明、江永、江电、江飞、江苏、江利、江天等8艘轮船。这是第一批由广州民办工厂制造的轮船。这批轮船造成下水,打破了帝国主义垄断珠江航运的局面。

"黄鹄"号
Huang Hu

19世纪60年代"中国最大的石船坞"
"China Largest Stone Dock" in 1860's

船舶修造是甲午战争前外资最重要的工业，集中在广州和上海两地，以19世纪四五十年代为初创期，六十年代以后为发展期，并逐渐出现少数大企业垄断的局面。

远洋航船到埠，必须检修，铁壳船必须淡水冲刷。在广州珠江的黄埔，早就形成中国手工造船中心，都是采用泥坞。早期外商帆船进口，都在这里检修；轮船初兴后，也是在泥垢洗修。大英轮船公司曾派苏格兰人柯拜（John Couper）驻广州管理船只入坞修理工作，他租了几个中国泥坞，并于1845年建立了一座新坞，这个柯拜船坞（Couper Dock）可算作外资在华开设的第一家工厂，也是中国近代造船工业的开端。

在广州，除柯拜外，有美商旗记铁厂（Thos.Hunt & Co.1851年），英商于仁船坞公司（Union Docks Co.1852年），诺维船厂（J.Rowe）；高阿船厂（Gow & Co.）和福格森船厂（Fenguson & Co.）等。

1.2. 柯拜船坞
Couper Dock

3.黄埔船坞：这是从长洲岛远望黄埔的全景，海港内侧停泊了美国和法国的商船，海港后面是黄埔岛，岛上可见岸边的仓栈及远方市镇的古塔
Whampoa Dock

洋商洋船的年代
The age of the foreign merchant ships

美国蒸汽机明轮船"河鸟"号（River Bird），该客货两用船于1854年下水，1855年夏天至1856年冬天行走于香港和广州之间。

American steam paddle steamer "dipper" (River Bird) is used both for passenger and cargo. It was put into use in 1854 and travelled between Hong Kong and Guangzhou from summer of 1855 to winter of 1856.

"河鸟"号
River Bird

1884年，张之洞出任两广总督后，订造了"广甲"等一批大舰，广甲号巡洋舰是福州船政于19世纪建造的一条铁胁木壳船，全长67.66米，宽度10.27米，排水量1300吨。

In 1884, Zhang Zhidong served as viceroy, made "wide" and a number of large ship, a wide cruiser is a wooden hull iron stress Fuzhou ship building built in the 19th century, the ship was 67.66 meters long, and 10.27 meters wide with a displacement of 1,300 tons.

1. "广甲"号
Guang Jia

2. 轮船招商局汽轮
Steamship of China Merchants Steamship Navigation Company

3. 美商旗昌公司"徽州"轮（1862年）航行广州至波士顿
Huizhou of Russeil & Co. (1862) from Guangzhou to Boston

4. 德忌利轮船公司"海清"轮航行香港至台湾
Hai Qing of Douglas steamship company sailing from Hongkong to Taiwan

1. 美商美孚火油公司"美峡"轮运油进入内地
Mei Xia of American Mobil Oil Company of round of oil into the mainland

2. 英商省港澳轮船公司"金山"号在广州
Jin Shan of the British Hongkong and Macau Ferry Company in Guangzhou

3. 大阪商船株式会社"香港丸"航行日港
Hong Kongwan of Osaka Shipping Corporation

1. 广东20世纪30年代内河渡轮
River ferry of Guangdong in 1930s

2. 广东西江"广平"号渡轮
Guang Ping in Xijiang, Guangdong

3. 民国时期新会县江门河上的船舶
The Xinhui County on the Jiangmen River, the Republic of China era

4. "中山舰"全景图（1926年）
Zhong Shan ship panorama (1926)

第三章 现代广东商船船型（1949年至今）
Modern Guangdong merchant ship (1949 – present)

新中国成立后，处于停滞状态的民族工业亟待恢复和发展，国内造船工业不仅关系到国民经济的发展，同时也是新中国海军建设的支柱产业。由于建国初期国内政治和经济的发展具有不同的时代特点，广东运输船舶也深深打上了时代的烙印。

After the founding of new China, the national industry in a stagnant state needs to be restored and developed. The domestic shipbuilding industry is not only related to the development of the national economy, but also the pillar industry of the construction of the new Chinese navy. As the early days of the founding of the domestic political and economic development has different characteristics of the times, Guangdong transport ship is also deeply marked with the imprint of the times.

艰苦创业——改革开放前
The start-up - before the reform and opening up

20世纪50—70年代初，珠江水系的货运船舶以拖驳船队为代表。这个时期，广东内河基本上仍使用新中国成立前遗留下来的蒸汽机拖轮，以木质居多，钢质甚少，比较著名的钢质蒸汽机拖轮以"大东风"为代表，其蒸汽机和锅炉的体积重量较大，拖带力强，可以拖带1000吨级货驳逆水上行西江，也是拖带广州5大客运航线（广州至梧州、肇庆、江门、三埠、石歧）花尾渡的主力。

1. 新中国成立初期—70年代初期，内河仍在使用前遗留下的蒸汽机拖轮
From the beginning of new China's foundation to the early 1970s, the steam tugs left were still used on the inland rivers

2. 经历20世纪半个多世纪的广东最具地方特色的平底木质客货驳船——花尾渡
Push-barge fleet of Xijiang River in 1960s, has characteristics such as a large volume, variety, and low cost of goods and low cost

3. 60年代西江顶推船队，具有运量大、运输货种多、成本低的特点
Push-barge fleet of Xijiang River has a characteristics such as large volume, transport of goods, and low cost

4. 60年代西江运煤顶推驳船组
The Xijiang River Coal barge in 1960s

1. 60年代出海的木帆船
Wooden masted boat in 1960s

2. 60年代广东自行设计制造的内河"红星"号钢质客船，220个卧位，平均吃水1.6，单机、单螺旋桨，航速约19公里/小时
Hong Xing , an inland steel passenger ship was designed and built by Guangdong with 220 berths in 1960s

3. 60年代新型客轮在梅州——潮州航线，汕头船厂设计建造90客位和115客位沿海短程客货船
New passenger liner in Meizhou – Chaozhou route, Shantou shipyard built 90 class and 115 class coastal short – range passenger ship in 1960s

1. 穗琼线客货轮（1964—1969年），"红卫"系列客货船，文冲船厂建造，沿海航行柴油机客货船，钢质，双桨，为广东建造的第一艘沿海钢质客货船，载客525人，载货250吨
Spike Joan line passenger cargo ship (1964 – 1969), Hong Wei series of passenger and cargo ships, Wen Chong shipyard built, Guangdong construction of the first ship coastal steel passenger ship, carrying 525 people

2. "琼沙"客货轮（1997年）航行于西沙群岛，广州造船厂建造，为三桨，双舵，可载219人，载货200吨，载淡水150吨，续航能力3000海里，自持力12昼夜。
Qiong Sha passenger cargo ship in Paracel Islands in 1977 was built by Guangzhou shipyard with a capacity of 219 seats

3. 70年代珠江250客客轮
250-passenger ferry on the Pearl River in 1970s

1. 70年代水泥船三年自然灾害，国家资源紧缺，同时为了减少木材使用，国家大力推广钢丝网水泥船的发展，在60年代、70年代，水泥船在广东得到了很好的发展和应用。
Cement ship have been well developed and used in Guangdong in 1960s and 1970s

2. 70年代珠江拖驳作业
Pearl River barge operations in 1970s

3. 沿海800吨货轮（1966年）新中国成立后广东早期批量生产定型船舶
The cargo ship with 800 tons in 1966 is the early volume production in Guangdong after the Republic of China

1. 广东远洋公司成立的第一艘"光华"轮，1961年赴印尼接难侨
The first Guang Hua ship established by Guangzhou Ocean Shipping Company went to Indonesia to pick up Chinese refugees in 1961

2. 1966年交通部、省政府授予在抗美援越中做出突出贡献的"1018"轮"南海英雄船"光荣称号
In 1966, the Ministry of Transportation, and the provincial government awarded the "1018" as the "Hero Boat of South China Sea" for its contribution to Aid Vietnam

3. 广远"黎明"轮1968年4月首次绕行台湾海峡
Guangyuan Li Ming steamship sailed around the Taiwan Strait for the first time in April 1968

中篇 图说广东商船船型变迁

1. "辽阳"号（1971年，13000吨）华南地区第一艘万吨远洋货轮
Liao Yang, the first ocean-going freighter with 13,000 tons in South China, 1971

2. "红旗121"轮，1976年开辟穿越台湾海峡的南北航线
Hong Qi 121 steamship opened the north-south route across the Taiwan Strait in 1976

3. 广州海运局油轮"大庆216"（1977年）船长106.07米，船宽14.94米，型深7.92米，满载吃水6.88米
Guangzhou Maritime Bureau tanker Da Qing 216 (1977), was 106.07 meters long, 14.94 meters wide, 7.92 meters deep, and with a draft of 6.88 meters

1. 1976年建造广远的汽车滚装船"康安口"轮
The construction of a great car ro-ro ship Kang Ankou in 1976

2. 60年代广州造船厂（水彩画）
Guangzhou shipyard (watercolor) in 1960s

扬帆起航——改革开放20年
Sailing – 20years of the reform and opening-up

党的十一届三中全会以后，我国进入了新的发展时期，坚持以经济建设为中心，国家实力迅速增强。广东船舶逐步从封闭走向开放，立足国内，面向世界，不断扩大与世界航运和造船界的交往，面貌发生了巨大的变化，取得了显著成就。随着内河客运的兴起，尤其在珠江三角洲经济高速发展的地区，客源逐年增加，广东内河客运船舶发展迅猛，广东沿海客货运输更是得到了空前的发展。随着国家社会经济的日益发展，钢材的逐步市场化，同时船舶建造的吨位越来越大，水泥船的劣势逐步显现，到20世纪80年代中后期，随着中国外贸运量的增加，特别是广东作为中国改革开放后商品进出口的重要口岸，提高运力势在必行，开始大量建造万吨级货轮，集装箱货轮及沿海油轮发展迅速，也取得了长足的进步。

1. 5000吨沿海货轮"红旗088"（1981年）华南地区建造以柴油机为动力的第二代海洋运输船舶
Hong Qi 088, a costal cargo ship with 5,000 tons was the second generation ocean transport ship powered by diesel engine in South China

2. 第一艘出口集装箱船（1981年，11,100吨），首次采用外国规范及相关国际规则
The first container ship with 11,100 tons firstly adopted foreign standards and relevant international rules in 1981

3. 第一艘出口散货船（1982年，18,000吨），华南第一艘万吨级出口散货船
The first million tons bulk cargo ship with 18,000 tons in 1982 in South China

4. 1983年首艘穿越台湾海峡的国内客轮"紫罗兰"号
In 1983, the first domestic ferry across the Taiwan Strait Zi Luolan

1. 1985年，广州海运局从希腊造"红棉"号和"红菊"号滚装客货轮2艘。其中"红棉"号为1500吨载货吨，476客位，可载60辆小汽车，主要航行于广州至海南航线
In 1985, Hong Mian and Hong Ju ro-ro passenger and cargo ships of Guangzhou Marine Bureau were manufactured by Greek. The main route is from Guangzhou to Hainan

2. 1986年文冲船厂建造的万吨级远洋教学实习船"育龙"号
Yu Long, a 10,000-ton ocean-going and teaching practice ship was manufactured by Wenchong shipyard in 1986

3. 90年代广东自行建造的第一艘双尾客轮"荣华"号，该轮为单头双尾、双机、双桨，设有2人和4人空调房间共52个卧位，大统舱300个卧位，配有空调餐厅
The first double tail ship built by Guangdong is called Rong Hua, which has a double-turbine and double-scull, and it is equipped with 2 and 4 air-conditioned rooms, a total of 52 berths, and a lounge with air conditioning

1. 黄埔船厂建造的162客位全铝合金高速船（1992年）
High speed ship made of full aluminum alloy with a capacity of 162 seats was manufactured by Huangpu shipyard in 1992

2. 90年代港澳客船
Hongkong and Macau passenger ship in 1990s

3. 粤中船厂1982年建造的500立方米对开式泥驳
500 cubic meters hopper barge was manufactured by central Guangdong shipyard in 1982

4. 1978年建造的广远子母船"沙河口"
Sha Hekou, a Guangyuan LASH(lighter aboard ship) was built in 1978

1. 1990年建造的广海38000吨级杂货轮"碧华山"轮
Bi Huashan, a Guanghai 38,000-ton cargo ship was built in 1990

2. 1978年建造的广州远洋公司的19000吨级散装木材船"云岭"号
Yun Ling, a 19,000-ton bulk timber ship of Guangzhou Ocean Shipping Company was built in 1978

3. 文冲船厂1981年建造的5000吨级远洋货轮
The ocean-going cargo ship with 5,000 tons was manufactured by Wenchong Shipyard in 1981

1. 80年代江南船厂建造的油轮"柳河"轮
   Liu He, a tanker was manufactured by Jiangmen Shipyard in 1980s

2. 1984年建造的广远"汤泉"轮
   Guangyuan Tang Quan was built in 1984

1. 广远"银河"号集装箱船（1984年）
Guangyuan Yin He container ship (1984)

2. 725TEU集装箱轮"隆河"号（1992年）是广州远洋公司首次在国内订造万吨级集装箱轮，也是华南地区跻身国内集装箱船制造先进地区的标志
725TEU container ship Long He (1992) of Guangzhou Ocean Shipping Company was the first million-ton container ship manufactured in China and also a symbol of South China to rise to the domestic advanced container ship manufacturing areas

3. 1200TEU集装箱轮"汉莎"系列（1995年）华南地区首次建造和出口欧美发达国家的万吨级具有国际先进水平的全集装箱船
Han Sha series in 1995, a 1200TEU container ship is internationally and first manufactured in South China and exported to European and American developed countries

驶向大海——进入新世纪
To the sea – enter into the new century

20世纪90年代后期,中国改革开发的步伐明显加快。特别是进入新世纪以来,全球经济一体化进程加快,国际贸易日益广泛,这些都要求船舶运输业能够跟上经济发展的步伐,中国船舶得到快速发展。2010年,中国世界造船份额位列世界第一位,已能够自主设计建造30万吨级超大型原油船和8000箱级超大型集装箱船,并已成功进入液化天然气船建造市场,打破了少数国家的垄断。目前,除豪华游船等少数船型外,中国已经能够建造符合各种国际规范,航行于任何海域的船舶。作为中国三大船舶基地的广东船舶也呈现出良好的发展势头,三大主力海运船型的散货船、集装箱船、油轮都朝大型化方向发展,珠江水系也正逐步形成江海联运、水陆联运的综合水运体系。

广东南沙港内河定期班轮"华航808"4500吨级集装箱船(2013年),也是目前西江水系最大内河集装箱船,可以装载集装箱210标箱
Regular liner of Guangdong inland river of Nansha port "Hua Hang 808" is a 4, 500-ton container ship in 2013, and also a current largest inland river container ship of Xijiang River with a capacity of 210 TEUs

1. 1700TEU集装箱轮系列船（2002年）是华南地区在国内乃至世界同类型集装箱船中最成熟、最先进的具有代表性的作品。该船型已经制造出批量达近40艘，出口德国、英国等国家
1700TEU container ship series in 2002 is the representative of the most mature and advanced container ship of South China at home and aboard. Nearly 40 ships have been manufactured to export to Germany and Britain

2. 目前最大散货轮"中海兴旺"（2009年，230,000吨）是华南地区目前制造的最大型散货船。本船是一艘远洋航行、单桨、单柴油机驱动的矿砂船，它适合载运矿砂并可以同时载运煤
Zhonghai Xingwang with 230,000 tons in 2009 is the largest bulk carrier in South China at present. The ship is an ocean-going, single-propeller, single-engine-driven ore vessel that is suitable for carrying ore and coal

3. VLCC"新浦洋"轮（2009年，308,000吨）华南地区目前制造的最大型巨型油轮。本船是一艘远洋航行、单桨、但柴油机驱动的原油船，它适合运载闪点低于60℃的原油
Xin Puyang (308,000 tons, 2009) is the largest supertanker in South China at present. The ship is an ocean-going, single-propeller, but diesel-powered crude oil tanker, which is suitable for carrying crude oil with a flash point below 60℃

1. 广州文冲船厂有限公司建造的2800TEU集装箱船"OS ANTALYA"轮（2007年），该船总长212.6米，型宽32.2米，型深20.3米，设计吃水10.5米
2800TEU container ship OS ANTALYA was built by Wenchong Shipyard Co. Ltd, Guangzhou with 212.6 meters long, 32.2 meters wide, 20.3 meters deep and a draft of 10.5 meters

2. 我国首艘LNG运输船"大鹏昊"，由沪东中华造船（集团）有限公司承建（2008年）。2008年5月2日，广东大鹏液化天然气有限公司在其秤头角接收站迎来了第一艘由中国制造的液化天然气（LNG）运输船"大鹏昊"。至此，"大鹏昊"圆满完成了它在澳大利亚—中国之间2700英里的LNG运输航线上的首航任务
Da Penghao, the first transport ship in China, was built by the Hudong Zhonghua shipbuilding (Group) Co. company (2008). On May 2, 2008, transport ship Da Penghao, Guangdong Da Penghao LNG Ltd in its Cheng Tou Jiao terminal ushered in the first Chinese made from liquefied natural gas (LNG)

蔚蓝船说 —— 广东商船船型变迁

21世纪海上丝绸之路与广东航运丛书 二

1. 2014年珠海高栏港迎来世界最大LNG（液化天然气）运输船型Q-Max船"阿萨利（AI Samriya）"号。这艘船体比"辽宁"号航空母舰还要长的巨无霸来自卡塔尔，船长345米，船宽54米，是广东省有史以来靠泊的最大LNG船舶
Zhuhai Gaolan Port had got the world's largest LNG (liquefied natural gas) transport ship Q-Max ship A Sali (Al Samriya). This ship was from Qatar, 345 meters long and 54 meters wide, which is the largest ever LNG ship in Guangdong province in 2014

2. 2014年12月，广州港南沙港区迎来了当今全球最大集装箱船"中海环球"号，全长400米，宽近60米，排水量为186,000吨，满载吃水达16米，船的水面高度为69米，有23层楼房高，19100的载箱量
In December 2014, Nansha Port ushered in today's world's largest container ship Zhonghai Huanqiu, which was 400 meters long, nearly 60 meters wide, with a displacement of 186,000 tons, a draft of 16 meters. The water surface elevation of the ship was 69 meters high as a 23- story building with a carrying capacity of 19,100 tons

3. 珠海建太阳能环保双体船（2009年），船长24米，船宽6米，满载吃水1.25米，它由风能、电能、太阳能及机器动力组成的混合能量驱动，可以说是目前世界上最先进的环保船。
Solar-powered catamaran was built in Zhuhai in 2009, which was 24 meters long, 6 meters wide and with a draft of 1.25 meters. The catamaran is said to be the most advanced green ship in the world at present since it was driven by a mixture of the wind energy, electric energy, solar energy and machine power

1. 中海油珠海船舶服务公司建造的国内首艘LNG双燃料港作拖轮"海洋石油521"（2013年），该船为双燃料发动机推进，可使用船用轻柴油（0#）、LNG气体作为燃料，设有2个容积为25立方米的LNG罐。
Haiyang Shiyou 521, the first domestic LNG dual fuel tugboat was built by CNOOC Zhuhai Shipping Service Company in 2013. This tugboat was powered by light diesel (0#) and LNG gas, and equipped with two LNG tanks with a capacity of 25 cubic meters

2. 2015年2月由广船国际制造的全国最大半潜船（72,000吨），船体长216米、宽63米，甲板长197米，半潜入水中26米，装货甲板面积达到12,400平方米，相当于1.7个标准足球场的面积
In February 2015, the largest semi-submersible (72,000 tons) of China was built by Guangzhou Shipyard. The hull was 216 meters long and 63 meters wide. The deck was 197 meters long and half-sneaked into the water. The loading deck area reached 12,400 square meters, which equals to the area of 1.7 standard soccer fields

第四章 珠江船型变迁
The change of the Pearl River ship

广州珠江
Guangzhou Pearl River

珠江是西江、北江、东江的总称，其中西江为珠江干流，长2129公里。珠江流经广州南面的江中，有一石岛。由于石岛长期受江水冲刷，其表面变得非常光滑，形似圆珠，当地的人们称它为"海珠石"，其长133米，宽50米，俨然一座小岛，故又称海珠岛，珠江由此得名。

1. 广州珠江景色（清代）
Guangzhou Pearl River scenery

2. 海珠岛（1909年）
The Island of Haizhu, 1909

广州珠江
Guangzhou Pearl River

1. 17世纪广州珠江
The Pearl River in the 17th century

2. 日伪时期广州珠江
The Pearl River in puppet period

1. 民国广州珠江
The Pearl River in the Republic of China

2. 现代珠江
The Pearl River today

海珠桥
Haizhu Bridge

  海珠桥是广州市第一座跨江桥，于1929年12月动工，1933年2月建成通车，由美国马克敦公司承建，称之为"珠江大铁桥"。当时的桥长180米，宽18.3米，为简文拱形下承钢桁架梁，以其临近"海珠石"改名为"海珠桥"，旧海珠桥为开合式桥梁，方便船只通过。

  1933年2月15日下午1点，万首翘望的海珠桥开通。海珠桥由马克敦公司建造，建桥的桥身用西门子马丁铜1700吨，从外国造好架子用船运往广州装配。大桥各留3.3米来做人行道，桥体可承重20吨的货车。开合式大桥最关键的是中间有个开合器，能够把两侧桥体升高。

On February 15, 1933, Haizhu bridge went into operation. Built by Makedun Company, retractable bridge is the key to a switching device, can be put on both sides of the bridge.

海珠桥旧照片
The old photo of Haizhu Bridge

1. 1938年10月，日寇要入侵，中国军队奉命炸毁桥，可是炸药不够，只炸坏了一点，从此，海珠桥也沦入魔掌之中。开合机器整套被日本人用船运回国去了。从此大桥不可以开舍，只能让小船通过，大船则泊于黄埔码头。后虽经修建，中段桥面开合部分已无法复原
In October 1938, the Japanese invaders were invaded, and the Chinese army was ordered to blow up the bridge, but the explosives were not enough to blow up a little. Since then, Haizhu Bridge has fallen into the clutches. The whole machine was opened and shipped by the Japanese. Since then the bridge cannot be open, but can only let the boat go through. The ship is parked at Whampoa. After the construction, the middle section of the bridge opening and closing part still can not be recovered

2. 1949年10月，解放大军南下之际，国民党军奉命炸桥。用了100箱炸药，在下午5点多把桥炸毁了。轰隆一声，珠江两岸的小船100多艘和蛋家3000多人，通通毁于江底，鲜血把珠江水染红了。钢铁大桥被炸得粉身碎骨，沉在水波中。一个小时后，解放军进入广州
In October 1949, the Nationalists troops were ordered to blow up the bridge while the People's Liberation Army moved southward. An hour later, the People's Liberation Army stepped into Guangzhou

3. 1950年3月，大桥由湖南衡阳铁路局修复开工。11月7日，苏联国庆那天通车，虽然不能再开合，但南北交通恢复了，市长叶剑英亲自剪彩
In march 1950,the bridge was repaired by the Hunan Hengyang Railway Bureau and opened on Soviet Union's National Day on 7 November. The north-south traffic recovered and the mayor Ye Jianying personally cut the ribbon

1. 20世纪60年代的海珠桥，中段桥身还有那个年代的标语"支援农业大跃进，全体人民有责任"
Haizhu Bridge in 1960s. The middle of the bridge there is the slogan of that era "to support the agricultural leap forward, all the people have the responsibility"

2. 20世纪80年代初扩建后的海珠桥
Haizhu Bridge Haizhu Bridge after expansion in early 1980s

3. 今日海珠桥
Haizhu Bridge today

大沙头与太古仓码头
Da Sha Tou and Tai Gu Cang Wharf

20世纪20年代初,孙中山政权辖下的航空局便设在大沙头,革命军政府制造的第一架战斗机"乐士文一"号也是在大沙头机场首度起飞,这个曾起飞过革命的飞机、担当广州水运枢纽角色的地方,已经发展成为具有广州滨水风情特色的旅游休闲胜地。

孙中山与夫人在飞机前合影留念,并亲自题写了"航空救国"四字以资鼓励
Sun Zhongshan and his wife inscribed "Aviation Salvation" for encouragement

1. 旧时大沙头码头
Da Sha Tou Wharf in old days

2. 今日大沙头码头
Da Sha Tou Wharf today

　　大沙头码头对于广州人来说，可以称得上是"水上的白云机场"。大沙头客运站由解放初期的40多家私营船务行于1954年3月组成联营，1956年3月全行业实行公私合营合并而成。大沙头客运站曾经是广州连接珠江流域沿岸各大、中、小城镇的水路客运始发点和终点。由于九十年代中后期水路客运受陆路客运飞速发展的影响，大沙头客运站逐渐取消了各条航线，转型为以珠江游为主的旅游码头，现在的大沙头客运站是目前广州整体配套设施最完备的珠江游游客集散中心和最大的珠江游游船"母港"。2011年游客接待量超过100万人次，占广州市珠江游游客接待量的一半以上，是广州市集旅游、娱乐、购物、餐饮于一体的最具特色的全开放式的滨江休闲胜地，堪称广州"外滩"。

　　太古仓码头位于广州市海珠区（旧称白蚬壳），由英国太古洋行于1904年—1908年间修建，供太古轮船公司使用，在当时是比较完善的仓储码头。2010年11月12日17时55分，"亚奥理事大家庭"号（"南海神"号）游船从太古仓码头徐徐起航，引领代表45个国家和地区的45艘花船，奏响了第16届广州亚运会开幕式的序曲——"一江欢歌"珠江巡游。

1. 大沙头码头夜景
 Da Sha Tou Wharf's night

2. 民国太古仓码头
 Tai Gu Cang Wharf in the Republic of China

3. 今日太古仓游艇码头
 Tai Gu Cang Marina today

珠江轮渡
Pearl River Ferry

广州被珠江分隔成三个自然块，即俗称的河北、河南及芳村。三区之间的交通最初是靠渡船，20世纪60年代初期，轮渡开始出现，不过当时的轮渡仍然是一种小型木质船，还要靠烧木炭、煤球来发动机器，载客量小、速度慢，也使用花尾渡载客。60年代末期，渡船开始使用钢丝网水泥船，载客量和过江速度都大大增加。1978年，广州轮渡有了钢壳船并一直沿用至今，渡江只需短短几分钟，各码头也从原始的简易木结构，逐渐改建为现代风格的两层混凝土结构。20世纪六七十年代轮渡被作为一种公益性的业务，费用不高，乘坐的人便不少，但利润很低，一直以来仅由广州市客轮公司经营。从1989年开始，客运量开始逐年递减，可以说，轮渡正在逐步走向消亡。其根本原因是交通的建设与发展。随着时间的流逝，跨江桥的数目逐渐增多，由1981年的三座，增加到了1989年的六座，而时至今天，已经有17座大桥横跨我们的"母亲河"了。公路已经很明显地取代了水路的地位。同时，交通工具的多样化，也对渡轮的经营造成一定的影响。

1921年以前，主要为横水渡、柱艇、沙艇等木质小船
Before 1921, Wooden boats were mainly cable ferry and sand boat

1. 花尾渡
Hua Wei ferry

2. 1978年"交远1"号，主要接代外宾的渡江游览钢壳船投入营运，到1984年钢壳船全部代替木壳船，钢丝网水泥船退役
Jiao Yuan No.1, the steel cruise ship for foreign guests was put into operation in 1978

3. 钢壳船的时代一直持续了三十几年。2013年12月，在1983年和1984年开始服役的7艘"铁壳仔"陆续退役，最后一艘"穗轮217"退役上最后一班岗时它仍相当平稳
The era of steel ships has lasted for over thirty years. December 2013, in 1983 and 1984 began to serve seven "iron shell Aberdeen" one after another retired, the last one "Sui Lun 217" retired on the last post when it is still quite stable

1. 2007年首条水上巴士航线芳村—中大航线开通，采用60客位"水上巴士"系列船舶
In 2007 the first water bus route in Fangcun opened, adopting "water bus" ships with a capacity of 60 seats

2. 岭南仿古风味玻璃钢199客位，设计航速约为12节，载客量为199客位，双舵双桨、双动力、液压操舵系统、机架合一操控系统（2013年）
The ship with Lingar flavor was made of glass and it was designed for the speed of 12 knots, with the capacity of 199 seats, and an integrated operational system of twin rudder oars, double drive, hydraulic steering system and a control system of the flame

1. 150客位，航速约为9节，载客量150客位，采用双舵双桨、双动力系统（穗水巴01船为单主机）、液压操舵系统、机架合一操控系统、闭式机舱设计（2014年）
Sui Shui Ba 01 with a capacity of 150 seats, 2014

2. 26.8米99客位玻璃铜船，设计航速约为12节，载容量为99客位，双主机动力系统、双发电机组、液压操舵系统、双舵双桨、机架合一操控系统（2014年）
The glass copper ship with a capacity of 99 seats, 2014

第五章 港澳航线船型变迁
Changes of Hong Kong and Macau ship

1. 澳门远眺及海港上的荷兰船只。1655—1657年间，荷兰派遣使节及东印度公司成员到中国洽商，海面可见两艘荷兰商船，其一正鸣炮致敬
Overlooking from Macau, and the Dutch ships on the harbor. Dutch ambassadors and members of the East India Company came to China to negotiate between 1655 and 1657, one of two Dutch merchant ships was showing respect with guns

2. 18世纪末的澳门，广州来的引航员在这里登上外国来华商船引航入广州
The pilots from Guangzhou boarded the foreign merchant ship in Macau at the end of 18th century

中篇 图说广东商船船型变迁

1. 香港中区及东区1860年时期的景色，欧式建筑在中区、半山一带密集，反映了当时港岛市容蓬勃发展的景象
This pencil scanning paintings depicting the central and Eastern Hongkong in 1860

2. 早期维多利亚城及山顶，香港总督府、圣·约翰堂等建筑，画面写实生动
The city of Vitoria and the Peak

3. 早期香港海上的帆船及快速帆船
Sailing boat and fast sailing boat on the sea of Hongkong

4. 清王朝道光二十年（1840年）鸦片战争爆发后，列强对中国开始了瓜分和掠夺，清政府被迫签订一系列不平等条约，香港被英国侵占，九龙被租借，新界被蚕食。广州至香港的航线，几乎全为洋商洋船所控制。图为美式蒸汽机明轮船"河鸟"号（River Bird），该客货两用船于1854年下水，1855年夏天至1856年冬天往返于香港和广州之间
The American Steam paddle steamer "dipper" (River Bird), the passenger and cargo ship launched in 1854, the summer of 1855 to 1856 winter walking between Hongkong and Guangzhou

蔚蓝船说——广东商船船型变迁

21世纪海上丝绸之路与广东航运丛书 二

1. 省港澳轮船公司最初是在1849年英商在香港成立的"香港广州轮船公司",以两艘小汽船行驶省港航线,1859年美国旗昌洋行与英商展开竞争,英国与葡萄牙船商于1865年联合组成"省港澳轮船公司",收购了美商及其他对手的全部船只,并增加广州、香港和澳门之间的航运,形成垄断局面。图是省港澳轮船公司"佛山"轮
Foshan steam ship of Hongkong - Macau Shipping Company

2. 省港澳轮船公司"泰山"轮停泊广州西堤
Tai Shan steamship of Hongkong - Macau Shipping Company

3. 省港澳轮船公司"西安"轮在广州码头
Xi'an, a steamship of Hongkong - Macau Shipping Company in Guangzhou port

中篇　图说广东商船船型变迁

1. 40年代航行广州—香港航线上的"武穴"号客轮
Wu Xue Ship for Guangzhou- Hongkong route in 1940s

2. 1979年首航广州—香港的豪华邮轮"星湖"号
Xing Hu's first voyage for Guangzhou - Hongkong route in 1979

3. 90年代港澳客船
Hongkong and Macau passenger ship in 1990s

1. 2014年2月17日起，广东省开始承担对从事广东省至香港、澳门航线普通货物运输的审批。这是交通运输部首次将港澳航线行政许可事项下放至省级交通运输主管部门。图是航行港澳航线的"方舟3"集装箱船，总长79.98m，型宽15.4米
Fang Zhou 3, a container ship for Hongkong - Macau route was 79.98 meters long and 15.4 meters wide

2. 图是航行港澳航线的"金龙112"散货船（总吨位4800吨）
Jin Long 112, a bulkcargo ship with 4,800 tons for Hongkong - Macau route

3. 航行港澳航线的"粤广州货0933"自卸砂船（总吨位2059吨）
Guangzhou 0933, a cargo ship loaded with sand with 2,059 tons for Hongkong - Macau route

4. 图是航行港澳航线的"穗航903"多用途船（总吨位1986吨）
Sui Hang 903, a multiple use ship with 1,986 tons for Hongkong - Macau route

中篇 图说广东商船船型变迁

1. 航行港澳航线的"玉茗100"油船（总吨位1845吨）
Yi Ming 100, an oil ship with 1,845 tons for Hongkong - Macau route

2. 航行港澳航线客船
The passenger ship for Hongkong - Macau route

3. 靠泊的港澳客船
Hongkong and Macau passenger ship is berthing

第六章 广东商船船型变迁大事记
Big Events of Merchant Ship Type Changes in Guangzhou

远古 Ancient Times	古文字中的舟船。 Boats in ancient writing.
新石器时期（4000年前） The Neolithic period (before 4000)	广东最古老的船舶历史，珠海高栏岛宝镜湾遗址岩画出现七艘渔船。 History of the oldest ship in Guangdong: seven fishing boats appeared in the site of Baojing Bay, Gaolan Island in Zhuhai.
新石器晚期 The late neolithic age	西汉南越王陵墓出土的船纹提筒有四艘环形船纹。 Unearthed from the tombs of king of Nan Yue in the Western Han Dynasty – ship grain bin has four ring ship line.
西汉 The Western Han Dynasty	广州西村皇帝岗出土木板船模。 Wooden ship model unearthed from the west village of Guangzhou.
东汉 The Eastern Han Dynasty	广州水阴路出土东汉陶船模（客船），出现世界上最早的舵和锚；广州红花岗出土东汉陶质模（货船）。 Ceramic ship model cargo ship unearthed from Guangzhou.
东晋末年 The Eastern Jin Dynasty	第一次采用水密隔舱技术的八槽舰。 The first use of watertight compartment technology in eight-boat ship.

唐代 The Tang Dynasty	楼船战船、木兰舟货船。 Towered warship and Mulan cargo ship.
宋元 Song and Yuan dynasties	南海一号、南宋车船、元海船。 Nanhai No.1, the southern Song Dynasty transport ship, Yuan ships.
明清 The Ming and Qing Dynasties	广东船、东莞大头船、新会尖尾船、乌艚船（白艚、乌艚）、福船、沙船、鸟船（绿眉毛）、红头船、米艇、大头艋（红单船）、七舨渔船、赶缯船、快蟹船、人字桅帆船、水师船。 The variety of the boats: Guangdong Ship, Dongguan Ship, Xinhui Rat-tail Ship, the boat ship (Bai Cao, Wu Cao), Fu Ship, Bird Ship (Lv Meimao), Red Head boat, Rice boat, Meng Ship (Hong Dan Ship), Qi Bang fishing boat, Gan Zeng boat, Fast Crab boat, Flip Ship, the navy ship.
1740年 1740	瑞典"哥德堡"号帆船。 Sweden Goteborg yacht.
1782年 1782	英国东印度公司船队。 The British East India Co fleet.
1784年 1784	美国"中国皇后"号。 American Empress of China.
1807年 1807	世界上最早出现的蒸汽机轮船。 The world's first steam ship.
1840年 1840	第一艘来自欧洲的汽轮船"复仇女神"号。 Nemesis, the first European steamship.
1841年 1841	脚踏渡船、紫洞船、画舫。 Ferry and pleasure boats.
1846年 1846	第一艘到达欧美的中国木帆船"耆英"号。 The first Chinese ship arrived in Europe and the United States Chinese wooden sailboat Qi Ying.
1845年—19世纪60年代	"中国最大的石船坞"，柯拜船坞。

1845 - 1960's	China's Largest Stone Dock, couper dock.
1850年	现存的三桅古帆船"金华兴"号。
1850	Jin Huaxing, the existing three masted ancient sailboat.
1855年	美式蒸汽机明轮船"河鸟"号。
1855	Dipper (River Bird), the American steam paddleboat.
1865年	我国第一艘蒸汽机轮船"黄鹄"号：
1865	Huang Hu, China's first steam ship.
1876年	第一艘由国内民营工厂生产的蒸汽机拖轮"江波"号。
1876	Jiang Bo, the first domestic tugboat manufactured by private plant.
1884年	"广甲"号巡洋舰。
1884	Guang Jia, the cruiser.
1899年	世界著名灯塔之一的湛江硇洲灯塔。
1899	Zhanjiang Island Lighthouse, one of the world famous lighthouse.
1908—1984年	广东客货运船舶"花尾渡"。
1908-1984	Hua Wei ferry, Guangdong passenger and cargo ship.
1926年	中山舰。
1926	Zhong Shan warship.
1940年	广州—香港航线上的"武穴"号客轮。
1940	Wu Xue, the passenger ship in the Guangdong - Hongkong route.
1947年	广州沿海航线的民营"剑门"客货船。
1947	Jian Men, privately operated passenger and cargo ship from Guangzhou.
1949年—1970年	蒸汽机拖轮。
1949 - 1970	Steam tugboat.
1960年	西江顶推船队、木帆船。广东自行设计制造的内河"红星"号钢质客船。
1960	Push-barge fleet, wooden masted boat of Xijiang River. Red Star, the steel passenger ship built by Guangdong.

1961年	广州远洋公司成立的第一艘"光华"轮，1961年赴印尼接难侨。
1961	Guang Hua, the first ship established by Guangzhou Ocean Shipping Company went to Indonesia to pick up Chinese refugees.
1964–1969年	广州到海南的"红卫"系列客货船。梅州—潮州航线汕头船厂设计建造90客位和115客位沿海短程客货船。
1964-1969	Hong Wei, passenger and cargo ship series from Guangdong to Hainan. Short-haul passenger and cargo ship was built by Shantou shipyard with capacities of 90 seats and 115 seats respectively.
1966年	新中国成立后 广东早期批量生产定型船舶沿海800吨货轮。交通部、省政府授予在抗美援越中做出突出贡献的"1018"轮"南海英雄船"光荣称号。
1966	After the founding of new China, Guangdong early produced mass of cargo ships with 800 tons. The provincial government awarded the "1018" as "Hero Ship of Nan Hai" for the outstanding contributions to the fight against OS.
1968年	广远"黎明"轮1968年4月首次绕行台湾海峡。
1968	Guangyuan Li Ming, travelled around Taiwan strait for the first time.
1970年	珠江250客豪华客轮、水泥船、珠江拖驳。
1970	The Pearl River luxury liner with a capacity of 250 seats, cement, and Pearl River barge.
1971年	华南地区第一艘万吨远洋货轮"辽阳"号（13000吨）。
1971	Liao Yang, the first ocean-going freighter with million tons in South China.
1976年	建造广远的汽车滚装船"康安口"轮。
1976	Kang Ankou, the construction of a great car ro ro ship.
1976年	"红旗121"轮开辟穿越台湾海峡的南北航线。
1976	Hong Qi 121 opened across the Taiwan Strait, North South route.

1977年	航行于西沙群岛的"琼沙"客货轮。广州海运局油轮"大庆216",船长106.07米,船宽14.94米,型深7.92米,满载吃水6.88米。
1977	The passenger and cargo ship "Qiongsha" sailed through the Xisha Islands. Da Qing 216, a tanker of Guangzhou Maritime. Bureau was 106.07 meters long, 14.94 meters wide, 7.92 meters deep and with a draft of 6.88 meters.
1978年	广州远洋公司的1.9万吨级散装木材船"云岭"号,广远子母船"沙河口"。
1978	"Yunling" of Guangzhou ocean, and "Shahekou" Guangyuan barge carries, 19,000 tons bulk timber ship.
1979年	首航广州—香港的豪华游轮"星湖"号。
1979	Xing Hu, First voyage Guangzhou - Hongkong luxury cruise.
1980年	黄埔、惠州、汕头及广州造船厂。
1980	Whampoa, Huizhou, Shantou and Guangzhou shipyard.
1981年	5000吨沿海货轮"红旗088"华南地区建造以柴油机为动力的第二代海洋运输船舶。
1981	Hong Qi 088 was a coastal freighter with 5000 tons was one of the second generation ocean transport ship using diesel engine as power in South China.
1981年	第一艘出口集装箱船(11,100吨),首次采用外国规范及相关国际规则。
1981	The first container ship with (11,100 tons) firstly adopts foreign standards and relevant international rules.
1982年	第一艘出口散货船(18,000吨),华南第一首万吨级出口散货船。500立方米对开式泥驳。
1982	The first million tons bulk cargo ship in South China (18, 000 tons for exports).
1983年	首艘穿越台湾海峡的国内客轮"紫罗兰"号。
1983	Zi Luolan, The first domestic ferry across the Taiwan Strait.

1984年	广远"银河"号集装箱船。广远"汤泉"轮敞货轮。油轮"柳河"轮。
1981	Liu He tanker; Guangyuan Tang Quan; Guangyuan "Yin He" container ship.
1985年	广州海运局从希腊造"红棉"号和"红菊"号滚装客货轮2艘。
1985	Hong Mian and Hong Ju ro-ro passenger and cargo ships of Guangzhou Marine Bureau.
1986年	文冲船厂建造的万吨级远洋教学实习船"育龙"号。
1986	Yu Long, a 10000-ton ocean-going and teaching practice ship was manufactured by Wenchong shipyard.
1990年	广海3.8万吨级杂货轮"碧华山"轮。
1990	Bi Huashan, a Guanghai 38, 000-ton cargo ship.
1992年	黄埔船厂建造的162客位全铝合金高速客船。广东自行建造的第一艘双尾客轮"荣华"号。
1992	
1992年	The first double tail ship built by Guangdong is called Rong Hua, which has a double-turbine and double-scull, and it is equipped with 2 and 4 air-conditioned rooms, a total of 52 berths, and a lounge with air conditioning.
1992	725TEU集装箱轮"隆河"是广州远洋公司首次在国内订造万吨级集装箱轮,也是华南地区跻身国内集装箱船制造先进地区的标志。 725 TEU container ship Long He of Guangzhou Ocean Shipping Company was the first million-ton container ship manufactured in China and also.
1995年	1200TEU集装箱轮"汉莎"系列华南地区首次建造和出口欧美发达国家的万吨级具有国际先进水平的全集装箱船。
1995	1200TEU container ship Han Sha series is the internationally advanced full container ship, which is firstly manufactured in South China and exported to European and American developed countries.

2000年	湛江、肇庆、清远、蛇口港。
2000	Zhanjiang, Zhaoqing, Qingyuan, Shekou, Whampoa port.
2002年	1700TEU集装箱轮系列船是华南地区在国内乃至世界同型集装箱船中最为成熟、最为先进具有代表性的作品。该型船已经制造出批量达近40艘，出口德国、英国等国家。
2002	1700TEU container ship series is the representative of the most mature and advanced container ship of South China at home and aboard. Nearly 40 ships have been manufactured to export to Germany and Britain.
2007年	广州文冲船厂有限公司建造的2800TEU集装箱船"OS ANTALYA"轮，该船总长212.6米，型宽32.2米，型深20.3米，设计吃水10.5米。
2007	2800TEU container ship OS ANTALYA was built by Wenchong Shipyard Co. Ltd, Guangzhou with 212.6 meters long, 32.2 meters wide, 20.3 meters deep and a draft of 10.5 meters.
2008年	广东大鹏液化天然气有限公司在其秤头角接收站迎来了第一艘由中国制造的液化天然气（LNG）运输船"大鹏昊"。
2008	Da Penghao, the first transport ship in China, was built by the Hudong Zhonghua shipbuilding (Group) Co. company. Transport ship "Da Penghao", Guangdong Da Peng LNG Ltd in its chengtoujiao terminal ushered in the first Chinese made from liquefied natural gas (LNG).
2009年	目前最大散货轮"中海兴旺"（230,000吨）华南地区目前制造的最大型散货船。本船是一艘远洋航行、单桨、单柴油机驱动的矿砂船，它适合载运矿砂并可以同时载运煤。
2009	Zhonghai Xingwang (230,000 tons) is the largest bulk carrier in South China at present. The ship is an ocean-going, single-propeller, single-engine-driven ore vessel that is suitable for carrying ore and coal.
2009年	VLCC"新浦洋"轮（308,000吨）华南地区目前制造的最大型巨型油轮。本船是一艘远洋航行、单桨、单柴油机驱动的原

	油船，它适合载运闪点低于60℃的原油。
2009	Xin Puyang (308,000 tons) is the largest supertanker in South China at present. The ship is an ocean-going, single-propeller, but diesel-powered crude oil tanker, which is suitable for carrying crude oil with a flash point below 60℃.
2009年	珠海建太阳能环保双体船，船长24米，船宽6米，满载吃水1.25米，它由风能、电能、太刚能及机器动力组成的混合能量驱动，可以说是目前世界上最先进的环保船。
2009	Nansha Port ushered in today's world's largest container ship Zhonghai Huanqiu, which was 400 meters long, nearly 60 meters wide, with a displacement of 186,000 tons, a draft of 16 meters. The water surface elevation of the ship was 69 meters high as a 23- story building with a carrying capacity of 19,100 tons.
2012年	英国"探险"号豪华邮轮顺利抵达广州黄埔港6号码头，350多名外国游客受到了热情欢迎。
2012	British explorer cruise ship arrived in Guangzhou Whampoa port pier 6, and more than 350 foreign tourists received a warm welcome.
2013年	广东南沙港内河定期班轮"华航808"4500吨级集装箱船，也是目前西江水系最大内河集装箱船，可以装载集装箱210标箱。
2013	Regular liner of Guangdong inland river of Nansha port Hua Hang 808 is a 4, 500-ton container ship, and also a current largest inland river container ship of Xijiang River with capacity of 210 TEUs.
2013年	中海油珠海船舶服务公司建造的国内首艘LNG双燃料港作拖轮"海洋石油521"。
2013	Haiyang Shiyou 521, the first domestic LNG dual fuel tugboat was built by CNOOC Zhuhai Shipping Service Company.
2014年	广州港南沙港区迎来了当今全球最大集装箱船"中海环

	球"号,全长400米,宽近60米,排水量为18.6万吨,满载吃水达16米,19100的载箱量。
2014	Nansha Port ushered in today's world's largest container ship Zhonghai Huanqiu, which was 400 meters long, nearly 60 meters wide, with a displacement of 186,000 tons, a draft of 16 meters. The water surface elevation of the ship was 69 meters high as a 23- story building with a carrying capacity of 19,100 tons.
2014年	珠海高栏港迎来世界最大LNG(液化天然气)运输船型Q-Maxt船"阿萨利(Al Samriya)"号。船长345米,船宽54米,是广东省有史以来靠泊的最大LNG船舶。
2014	Zhuhai Gaolan Port had got the world's largest LNG (liquefied natural gas) transport ship Q-Max ship A Sali (Al Samriya). This ship was from Qatar, 345 meters long and 54 meters wide, which is the largest ever LNG ship in Guangdong province.
2015年	由广船国际制造的全国最大半潜船(72,000吨)。
2015	The biggest national semi-submerged ship with 72,000 tons, manufactured by Guangzhou Shipyard International (GSI).
2015年	今日南沙港、盐田港。
2015	Nansha Port and Yantian Port today.
2015年	今日珠江夜游客船、仿古船。
2015	The Pearl River cruise ship and antique ship today.

下篇
广东航运文化
Shipping culture in Guangdong

第一章 牵星术与海图
The star drawing technique and the chart

《汉书·地理志》记下徐闻、合浦的梯航之路长3500～5300公里，唐贾耽记下的"广州通海夷道"长达14000公里。大海茫茫，船在海中航行要有参照物才不至于迷途。当在海上航行无山无屿时，就要利用日月星辰来判定船只所在位置，决定前进的路线。一年四季太阳的位置南北移动，白天东西转移，夜间繁星布空，北斗指路。这就是"牵星术"，它是航海人的经验总结。"牵星术"是中国土特产，早在战国时期，我国就有一套《巫成占》，可用以测量星体高度。汉唐宋有"指"、有"星经"还有不少"海上观星""观日月、潮汐、气象"等书。既能海上牵星，测定船位，也为后代元、明、清应用。"

据《古地图密码》云："北宋绍圣年间，张匡正墓后室的顶部也为穹窿形，一幅直径约为两米的图形星象图绘在顶部的正中央……星象图的外圈内用黑红色绘出太阳、月亮和其他一些主要恒星，二十八星宿按照投影法排列，各个星宿所处的方位几乎与中国传统的二十八宿星象图相差无几。""星象图的内圈为二十瓣莲花图案，象征着十二方位星象观测法。"可以想知，在宋代指南针与星象图的使用是促进和发展海外贸易的重要因素。

海图是航海的工具，利用海图航海是手段。在宋代的《诸蕃志》已有所述："暇日阅诸蕃图，有所谓'石圹''长沙'之险。"《海外诸蕃地理图》《郑和航海图》等都是实践过程中反复锤炼出来的，可以付之实用的航海工具。

有了日月星辰的认知，航海者利用牵星术日夜航行于海浪滔滔的大海；有了海图航海者又进了地理认知的大门。于是航海由初级阶段的梯航进入"夷道"，驶向更遥远的欧洲、非洲国家，将中国的丝绸、瓷器、茶叶等商品直接销往那里。

但是不可忘却，随着船只驶向南海深处，驶进印度洋，大海对船只的劈浪性能、安全性、稳性、船舶结构、造船材料、船舶配置等也提出了更高的要求。因此水密舱结构、上窄下宽的船型、多层船底板、舷侧扳、麻丝桐油石灰抡缝防漏、多变的帆以及坚实的木材等为保证安全航行被大量应用于船舶。

入宋后，罗盘仪用于航海，航海进入了初级科学阶段，更使航船如虎添翼，日夜航行中再配合海图，想去哪就开往哪儿，这是因为"舟师识地理，夜则观星，昼则观日，阴晦观指南针。"徐兢《宣和奉使高丽图经·卷三十四》曰："惟视星斗前进，若冥晦则刷指南浮针，以揆南北。"这是船与航海的相依关系。

有载体，善航海，并随着造船业的发展和航海线路的调整，我国的海外贸易鬼规模从小到大，港口众多，南北东西走向四方，亚洲、非洲、欧洲、南北美洲都有中国帆船的踪迹。

初时的海外贸易是一种赉赐、赐予贸易，是朝廷派使节或商人出洋，从事一些外交活动和商业活动，没有营利目的。被赐国受赐后也会遣使朝贡，两国互相往来。民间的航运贸易则是受到朝廷制约的，民间的贸易远不如官方的量大。

建唐后，由于政治清明、经济复苏与发展，贸易迅速开展，来往广州的船舶增长很快，据《新唐书·李勉传》："大历五年（770年），收泊广州的蕃舶竟达4千余艘之多。""贸易的国家地区不下100多个"，"咸通十一年（870年）到广州贸易的外国商人达到13万之多，开元时间，一年之中来往流动于广州的客商竟达80多万人次，其中的阿拉伯商人为多。"盛唐时期主要出口商品是丝绸织品。天宝年间，各国船舶盛况空前，据《唐大和尚东征记》曰：广州"江中有婆罗门、波斯、昆仑等舶，不知其数。并载香药、珍宝，积载如山。"

盛唐之后，经济发展迅速，中国成为世界经济大国，陶瓷生产量大、质量上乘，深受外国商人青睐。因唐来时期名窑陶瓷大量由海上丝绸之路输出，及丝织品、五金原料都销往国外。泉州、宁波的兴起，东西航线两翼齐飞，南往北来，中国的船舶满载国货扬威海外。海外贸易还不仅自运自销，还通过第三国转运转销，走海外贸易的另一条渠道。据史述，"出口菲律宾转运至拉丁美洲的商品有生丝、丝织品、线绢、瓷器、陶缸、铁锅、铁、铜、锡、铅、水银、砂糖、火药、棉布、花生、栗子、枣子、白纸、色纸、母牛、母马、火腿、咸猪肉、花边、安石榴、梨、橙、蜜饯、墨、珠子串等数十种。"转往墨西哥的大帆船，一次装丝货甚至达到1200箱。海外贸易线还延伸到果阿、里斯本，拉美线与里斯本的扩展使我国海上丝绸之路登上高峰期。

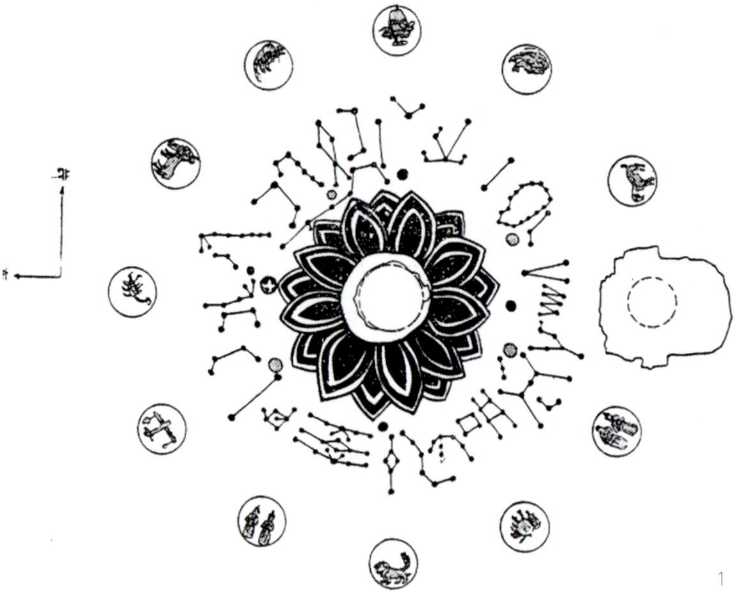

1

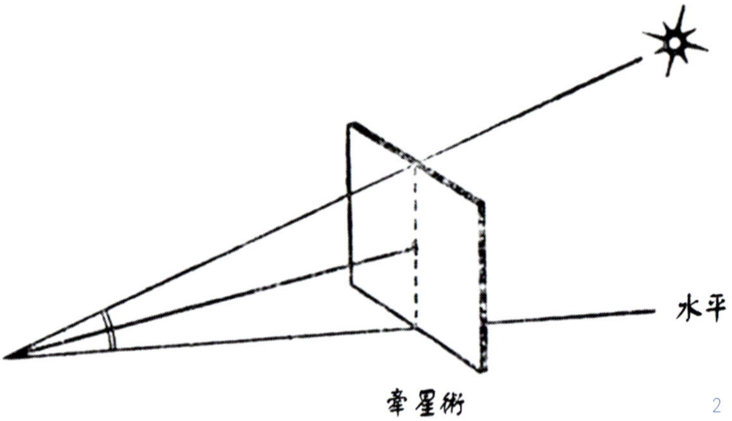

2

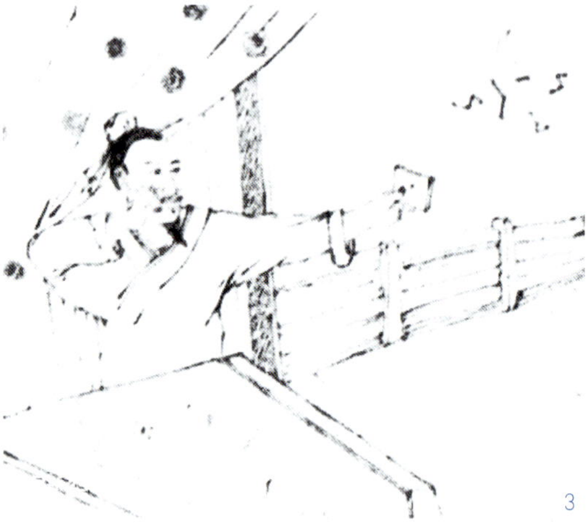

3

1. 北宋年间的星象图
Astrological chart in the Northern Song Dynasty

2.3. 牵星术
The star drawing operation

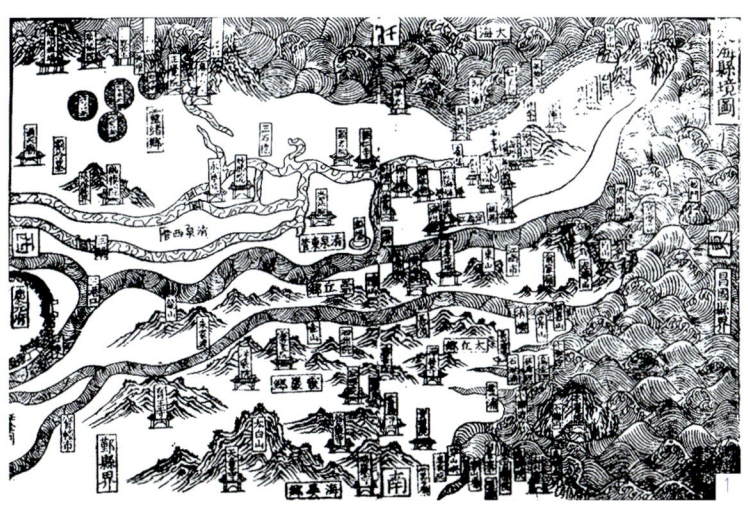

1. 诸蕃图
The overseas fan geographic map

2. 郑和航海图
Zheng He's nautical chart

　　《郑和航海图》原名是《自宝船厂开船从龙江关出水直抵外国诸蕃图》，因其名冗长，后人简称为《郑和航海图》。原图呈一字形长巷，收入《武备志》时改为书本式，自右而左，有序一页，图面二十页。

　　这本图集是世界上现存最早的航海图集。

"Zheng He" was originally called "off the charts is the effluent from Longjiang since the sail to the yard foreign Diophantine", because of its long name, later referred to as "Zheng He's nautical chart". The original figure was in the form of a zigzag, and was transformed to a book that had one page of preface and 20 pages of pictures when adopted into "Wubei Zhi".

第二章 广东人"下南洋"
Cantonese to the Southeast Asia

在中国近代史上，有三次大的移民潮，分别是闯关东、走西口、下南洋。下南洋可以追溯到汉代，但主要指的是明朝到清末。下南洋的人来自全国大部分省区，但以广东和福建人为主，目的地是东南亚一带。

下南洋
To the Southeast Asia

东南亚与中国山水相连，自古以来便是东南沿海百姓移居海外的主要目的地。早在秦汉时期，即有海商进入东南亚的记载。唐宋时期，中国海商遍布东南亚沿海地区，人口往来频繁。15世纪初，爪哇、苏门答腊等地出现华人聚居区。明中后期，政府多次发布禁令限制出海，但由于海外贸易的兴盛，前往东南亚的人口依然有增无减。然而，真正形成规模并影响至今的移民活动，则是近代以来称为"下南洋"的移民潮。

南洋包括今新加坡、马来西亚、印度尼西亚等东南亚11国。清代泛称"南洋"，后沿用至20世纪中期。17世纪以降，西方殖民势力开始进入远东地区，荷兰、西班牙、葡萄牙、英国等国家先后在东南亚开辟商埠，将远东地区纳入世界殖民贸易体系。开发东南亚急需大量劳动力，而非洲黑奴贸易在18—19世纪之交已经衰落，西方殖民国家开始把眼光投向人口众多的中国，颁布了一系列优惠政策，鼓励华人前往东南亚。就国内而言，闽粤自古以来便是海上贸易、对外移民活跃的地区，"闽广人稠地狭，田园不足于耕，望海谋生"。鸦片战争前，"下南洋"的华人以经商谋生者居多，当时东南亚华人已有150万之多。

晚清时期，清政府被迫签订种种不平等条约，包括允许西方在东南沿海招募华工，因为应募者要订立契约，名为"契约华工"，俗称"卖猪仔""当苦力"。由此，"下南洋"进入了一个新的时期，其过程大致可以分为两个阶段：

第一阶段：从1860年代至20世纪初，出现以华人劳工为主体的海外移民潮。1860年代，在经历太平天国、两广洪兵起义和广东土客大械斗之后，时值美洲发现金矿、东南亚种植园经济发展，各国纷纷设立招工公所，洋行、公所通过雇佣"客头"（猪仔头），将贫民诱至"猪仔馆"，签订契约，以出国后的工资为抵押，换取出洋旅费。1912年，中华民国临时政府颁布禁止贩运"猪仔"与保护华侨的法令，苦力贸易终结。

第二阶段：从20世纪初到50年代初，是"下南洋"的高峰时期。20世纪前期，中国国内兵连祸结，战火不断，而东南亚则得到殖民宗主国的扶持，除了传统的种植园、采矿业外，铁路、航运、金融、制造等新产业也获得空前发展，急需熟练劳工。二战后，迁往东南亚的华人大幅减少。新中国建立后，持续数百年的"下南洋"移民潮基本停止。

"下南洋"自明代中叶开始，在20世纪50年代戛然而止，持续近300年。俗话说"海水到处，就有华人"。海外华人华侨的总数，目前比较认可的数字是3500万，80%分布在东南亚，其中印尼华人数量最多，约有600万；马来西亚次之，有500万左右；华人占多数的唯一国家是新加坡，约占总人口的75%以上。

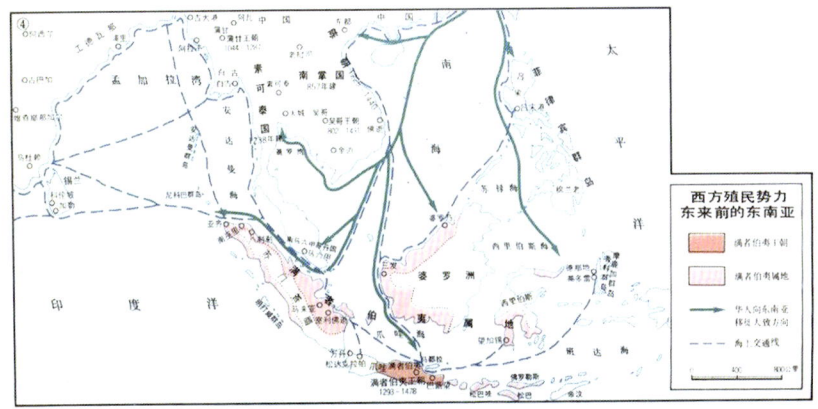

南洋
The Southeast Asia

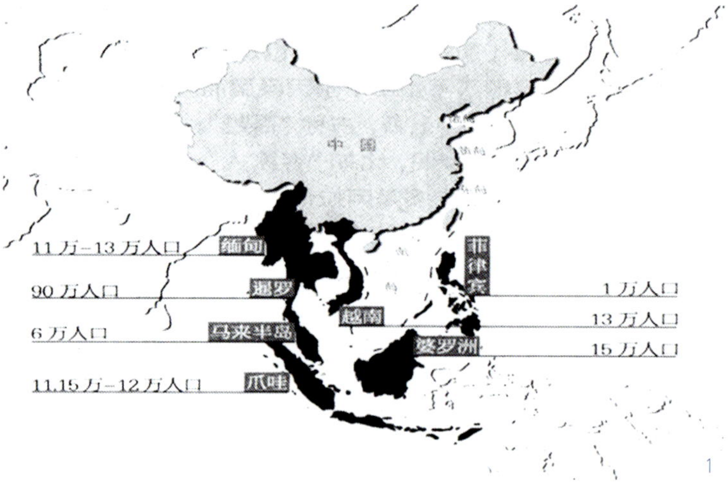

1. 19世纪华人下南洋的人员分布
The distribution of Chinese people in the 19th century

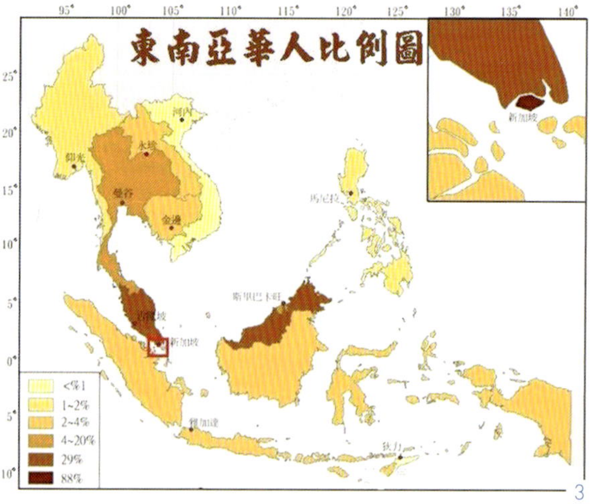

2 下南洋迁徙方向及聚居地.
Movement and settlement

3. 20世纪东南亚华人比例图
Ratio map of Chinese in Southeast Asian countries in the 20th century

下南洋的血泪史
The tragic history of sailing to the southest Asia

  首先是"违法"。移居海外在很长时期内是不允许的，在朝廷看来，迁居海外无异于"弃绝王化"，不仅禁止，而且对回国者严加制裁。直到晚清，清政府才意识到海外华侨的经济实力与商埠的重要性，于光绪三年（1877年）任命当地华侨领袖胡璇泽为新加坡首任领事。1893年，清政府才正式解除"华侨海禁"。

  其次是旅途艰险。早期移民偷渡出洋，整日担心官军稽查与海盗行劫，海上风信难测，帆船时时有倾覆之险。近代出洋华工则几乎与奴隶无异，饱受"猪仔头"与"猪仔馆"的虐待，华工被封禁在船舱内，条件恶劣，死亡率极高，贩运华工的船只被称为"移动地狱"。

  再就是落地后的艰难。落地移民一是要克服难以适应自然环境的问题，二是受到当地各种势力的多重压迫。大量华人移居东南亚，不仅缓解了中国国内的人口压力，也极大地推动了东南亚各国经济的开发与发展。东南亚的近现代历史是土著族群与华人共同书写的。

1. 当年贩卖"猪仔"的情景
The sale of Chinese

2. 16—17世纪运载中国货物和中国移民前往南洋的帆船
Sailing launch Chinese goods and Chinese immigrants to the Southeast Asia in the 16th-17th century

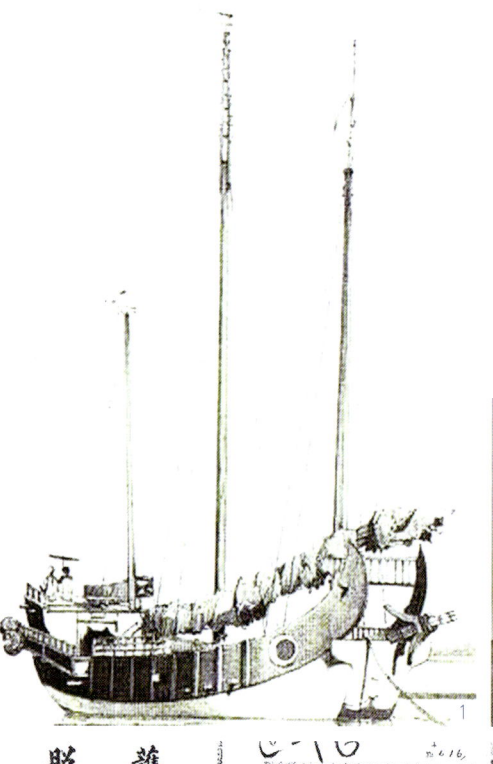

1.2. 南洋史料中，清道光年间到达新加坡的下南洋帆船
The ship to Singapore in the Qing Dynasty

3. 清政府签署的华商护照
The Chinese passport signed by Qing government

4. 马来西亚锡矿业早期发展几乎完全依靠华侨劳工和华侨资金
The early tin-mining development of Malaysia is almost depend on overseas Chinese and capital

1. 印度尼西亚咖啡园的华工
Chinese coffee garden laborers in Indonesia

2. 华人街贩和金饰匠蜡像，现存于菲律宾菲华历史博物馆
Chinese street vendors and Goldsmith wax figure, existing in Philippines Chinese History Museum

3. 100年前的印尼邦加契约华工之运输工具——手推车
Cart, Bangka contract laborers transportation 100 years ago

广东人下南洋
Cantonese to the Southeast Asia

郑和七下西洋都是途经广东省南海水域的南澳岛（今广东省南澳县）、七尖星（今惠东县东南的大洲岛）等地，然后到达西洋诸国，其中郑和第二次下西洋还是"首从广东往占城"的。而广东人向海外南洋移民正是在郑和下西洋后的明中叶逐渐形成"移民潮"的。明中叶以降，随着以商品流通为基础的贸易全球化的形成，和广东成为贸易全球化中心市场的有利条件，无数广东商人到南洋贸易，"往往久住不归……间有削发长子孙者。"同时，由于当时明廷实行海禁政策，造成部分走私商人逃避官兵追剿而移民南洋，从而形成了南洋移民热潮。当时广东人主要是向安南、占城、暹罗、北大年、马六甲、印度尼西亚、菲律宾、文莱等国家移民。

安南与广东的钦州、廉州（今属广西）山水相连，双边贸易历来十分频繁。由于生意兴隆，客居既繁，广东及各省商人在会安建立了天妃宫和会馆。占城位于安南之南，是一个商业贸易的重要枢纽。嘉靖年间（1522—1566年），安南屡起事端，侵扰占城，明朝支持占城，以牵制安南。

暹罗是广东商人移民的主要侨居地之一。明初已有南海人何八观等"流移海岛，遂人暹罗"。克路士的《中国志》称，有些广东商人到马六甲、暹罗、北大年等地做生意，就留居下来，"不再返回中国"。北大年是暹罗的属国，又称大泥，明中叶后期"华人流寓甚多"。16世纪70年代，这里已有一名华人拿督，对当地经济有相当大的影响。

广东商人侨居马六甲历史悠久，嘉靖年间（1522—1566年），南海人黄衷说马六甲"俗禁食豕肉，华人流寓或有食者，辄恶之，谓其厌秽也"。16世纪初，满刺加设有四个沙班达尔（Shahbandar），即港长、港务官之类，由中国人、爪哇人、束巴亚人及孟加拉人各一人担任，说明华人在满刺加受到重视和信任。1641年，马六甲华侨已有300~400人。

明初，爪哇灭三佛齐，然不能尽有其地，"华人流寓者往往起而据之"，"很多广东籍富商住在那里，其中有些已改信了伊斯兰教"。而这里的华人都是广东、福建两省的人。16世纪末，万丹华侨人口有3000~4000人之多。

明初苏禄国朝贡取道广州，有利于加强双边关系。西班牙人占领菲岛后，悉数与中国通商贸易，鼓励中国商民前往马尼拉贸易。广东商人运载各种商品到菲律宾，由当地商人分销，运回金银和其他外国产品。菲律宾华侨以广东、福建两省为多。崇祯八年（1635年），马尼拉涧内有华侨2万人以上，其他海岛约1万多人，全菲华侨达3万多人。

红头船是粤东（通称潮汕）地区和东南亚地区建造的广东海洋贸易商船，是典型的广船中晚清时期的代表。人们历来把红头船当作清代潮州从事远洋贸易的商船，大多数潮籍华侨就是乘坐红头船到海外谋生，寻求发展。红头船曾经是中国同世界各地经济和文化交流的纽带，也是各地华侨同祖国联系的纽带。每年趁季候风，红头船组成的庞大船队就会浩浩荡荡地扬帆远征，北上苏州、上海、宁波、青岛、天津，南下达雷州、琼州、越南、暹罗、新加坡及东南亚诸国。

由于海禁，清廷对造船有严格的限制，因此曾经是潮汕地区自造的红头船难以取得发展，也令广东的海上交通受到了制约。但是，华侨、商人在贸易中看到了东南亚国家的商机，以商人独到的获利眼光，以当时清廷正需要大量进口大米为的时机，以申请进口大米为契机，随同大米一起从南洋运回象牙、珠宝等奇珍异宝、贵重药材、当地特产等"压载物"。运往南洋的则是陶瓷、湖乡、雕刻件、蒜头、麻皮、菜籽、人参、鹿茸、兽皮、丝绸等受东南亚欢迎的货品，在泰国大量订造红头船。事实上，当时中国的木质帆船也是只能来往于东南亚——中国航线。红头船成了清代对东南亚贸易和国内重要贸易的主力。

1. 广东华工下南洋
Chinese workers of Guangdong to the Southeast Asia
2. 下南洋时不幸病倒船库，幸得同乡互相扶持，乡情满溢
Support each other while ill

蔚蓝船说——广东商船船型变迁

21世纪海上丝绸之路与广东航运丛书

1. 潮汕先民乘坐红头船过番
Chaoshan people Red Head Boat ride over time

2. 红头船出海场景
Red Head Boat in the sea

红头船

(电视剧《家园》主题歌)

1=D 4/4
每分钟60拍

陈洁明 词
程大兆 曲

5 6 1̇ 3·2 1 | 2̇ 3̇ 2̇ 1̇ 6 6 — | 5 6·1̇ 5 3· |
1. 天 连 着 海　　海 连 着 天　　离 别 家 园
2. 风 里 浪 里 常 聚 常 散　　但 求 情 深

5 6 5 2 4 3 — | 3·3 2 3 5 5 3 5 | 6·1̇ 2̇ 3̇ 2̇ 1̇ 6 — |
红 头 船　　为 了 过 上 好 日 子 好 日 子
有　 缘　　顺 风 流 水 又 顺 意 又 顺 意

5·6 1̇ 1̇ 2̇ 1̇ 6 | 2̇ 3̇ 5 2̇ 3̇ 1̇ — | 0 5 6 1̇ 3·2̇ 3̇ |
阿 哥 下 海 到 天 边 到 天 边　　红 头 船 近
阿 哥 一 路 保 平 安 保 平 安

0 5 6 1̇ 2̇·1̇ 6 | 0 5 3 5 6 1̇ 1̇ 6 1̇ | 2̇ 2̇ 3̇ 1̇ 2̇ 6 5 — |
红 头 船 远　　别 忘 了 阿 妹　　别 忘 了 家 园

0 5 6 1̇ 3·2̇ 3̇ | 0 5 6 1̇ 2̇·1̇ 6 | 0 5 3 5 6 1̇ 1̇ 6 1̇ |
红 头 船 近　　红 头 船 远　　心 里 有 个 岸

2̇ 2̇ 3̇ 1̇ 6 5 5·6 5 | 3·5 6 2̇ 3̇ | 2̇·3̇ 1̇ 5 6 6 — ‖
牵 挂 到 永 远 哎　　　　牵 挂 到 永 远.

2̇·3̇ 3̇ 3̇ 2̇ 1̇ | 1̇ — — — ‖
牵 挂 到 永 远.

《红头船》歌
The song of "Red Head Boat"

广东侨民对南洋的经济开发
Guangdong overseas Chinese for the Southeast Asian economic development

明中叶至清嘉庆年间（1550—1820年），中国是世界经济发达的国家，据统计，嘉庆二十五年（1820年），中国的GDP占世界经济总量的32.4%，居世界第一位。所以"在近代以前的时期的所有文明中，没有哪一个国家的文明比中国更发达，更先进"，"中国人有世界上最好的粮食——米，最好的饮料——茶，最好的衣料——棉布、丝织品及皮货。拥有这些主要物品和数不尽的其他次要的物产"。而南洋诸国则是经济欠发达的，有些国家尚待开发。所以，广东商人移民南洋各个国家和地区，既通过贸易运去无数中国的先进商品，供给当地人民的生活需要，又带去先进的生产工具和先进生产技术，为南洋各个国家和地区的经济开发提供了首要条件；而他们在与当地人民一起共同开发中亦做出了贡献，功不可没。

在爪哇的万丹，华侨大部分是经商，还种植水稻、胡椒和酿酒。在巴达维亚，广东华侨分别从事种植水稻、水果、胡椒、甘蔗等农业生产；从事榨糖、酿酒、榨油等农产品加工业。在安汶岛，广东侨民是"聪明、勤俭、亲切，而又善于谋利的国民。在菲律宾，华侨除经商外，他们"所做的工作是机匠、木匠、园丁、农夫及其他生产粮食的劳作"。广东华侨把中国先进的生产技术和经验带到南洋国家，对提高当地生产技术与经济水平起着重要作用。暹罗造船业、制瓷业在16—17世纪兴盛起来，很大程度上也是华侨积极参与技术上无私指导的结果。

总之，大批广东商民移居南洋诸国，从事各种各样的职业，对于相对落后或有待开发的南洋各国而言，既提供了大量的先进生产技术和年富力强的劳动人手，又带来了丰富的中国商品、资金和生产工具，成为推动南洋社会进步和经济开发的积极因素。与此同时，广东移民亦将中国的传统文化传播到南洋各国，对各国的文化起了交流和促进的作用。漂流海外的孤独感和受到的各种压迫，促使华人通过种种方式来保护自己、寻求慰藉与帮助，一是与土著通婚。二是创立同乡会馆。三是加入秘密会党。

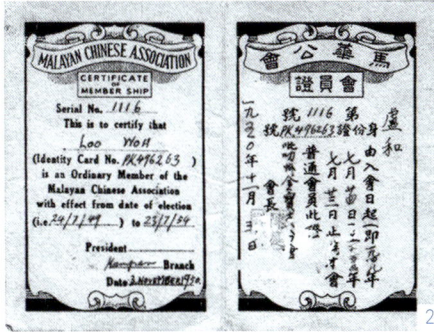
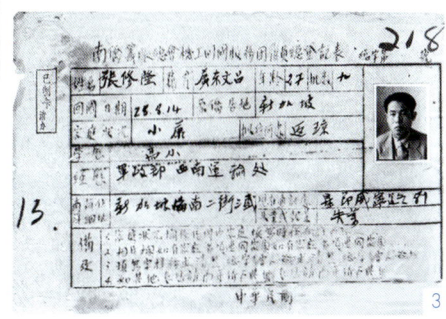

1. 马来西亚槟榔屿的中国城内建于1928年的中华总商会，记载着当年华人奋斗的历史
China city of Penang Island in Malaysia was built by Chinese Chamber of Commerce in 1928, recorded the history of the Chinese struggle

2. 20世纪40年代马来西亚华人政党马华工会的会员证
Membership card of Malaysia Chinese Party MCA in 1940s

3. 南侨机工
The overseas Chinese mechanic

4. 1940年，陈嘉庚率领南洋华侨归国慰劳视察团访问延安
Overseas Chinese led by Jiageng Chen visited Yan'an in 1940

1. 50年代初在雅加达港口欢送先期回国的同学。背景是回国同学乘坐的荷兰Cinangi（芝万宜）
Farewell to classmates at Jakarta port in 1950s

2. 往昔的清澜港（泰国侨领欧宗清的家庭藏相）
Qinglan harbor in the past

3. 1887年开业的新加坡梨春国戏院
Li Chun Theatre in Singapore in 1887

下篇 广东航运文化

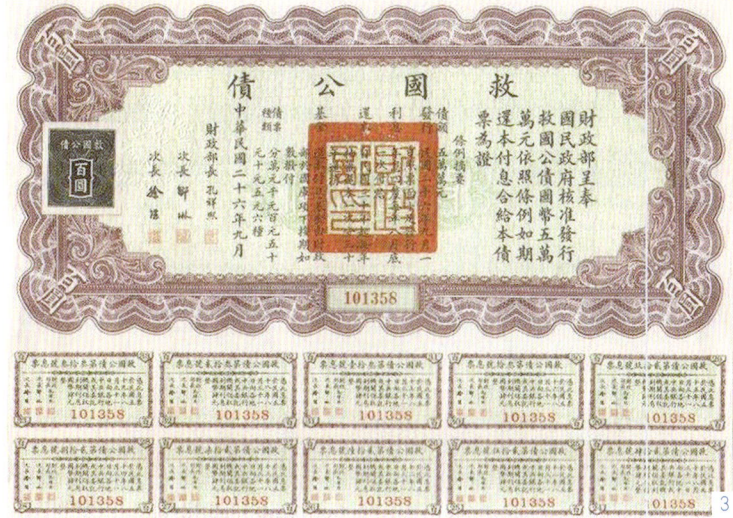

1. 东山下南洋华侨别墅
Overseas Chinese villa at the foot of Dongshan

2. 文昌南洋骑楼
Wenchang Southeast Asian Arcade

3. 在南洋发行的救国公债
National bond issued in the Southeast Asia

兰芳大统制共和国
Lan Fang Republic

兰芳大统制共和国（1776—1886年），通常简称兰芳共和国，是18世纪70年代到19世纪80年代之间存在于南洋婆罗洲（现印度尼西亚占据称加里曼丹岛）上的海外华人所创立的第一个共和国，也是亚洲历史上的第一个共和国。

乾隆三十七年（1772年），广东梅县（今梅州市区）的客家人罗芳柏与百余名亲戚朋友漂洋过海，来到盛产金矿和钻石的婆罗洲（即今印度尼西亚西部的加里曼丹岛）。起初，芳柏以教书为业，他有文化、有胆识、有才能，又懂武术，身体壮实，既能团结侨胞，又能与当地土人合作，深受当地人民和华侨的拥戴。罗芳柏在站稳脚跟后，积极联络苏丹和当地土族头人，成立华侨与当地民众相结合的军队，奋力击退外来入侵者，取得了东万律的管辖权。1777年，罗芳柏根据当地人民的意见，着手建立"兰芳公司"，在他管辖下的11万民众一致拥戴他，称他为"大唐总长"，敬称为"芳伯"。罗芳柏将"公司"改为"共和国"，以东万律为首都的"兰芳大统制共和国"建立。这一年定为兰芳元年。

芳伯名芳柏，清乾隆三年（1738年）出生于梅县石扇一耕读之家。
Fang Bai was born in Mei Country, 1738

下篇 广东航运文化

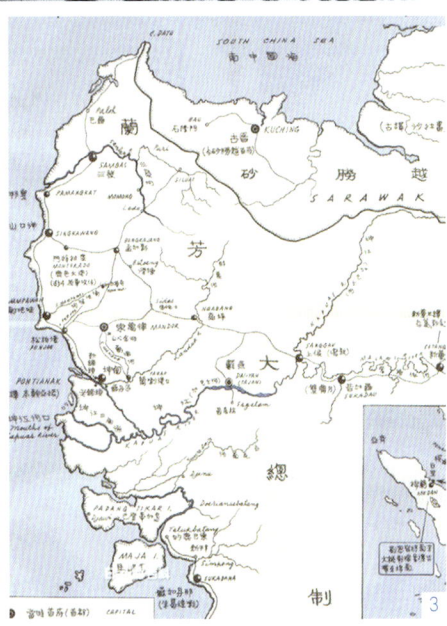

1. 乾隆四十二年（1777年），罗芳柏站在西婆罗州（今印度尼西亚的西加里曼丹有）东万律的"兰芳大总制"府邸前，接受弟兄们的朝贺
Congratulations to Fangbo Luo by his friends in the West Coast of Borneo in 1777

2. 兰芳大统制疆域
Lan Fang territory

第三章 "十三行"
Guangdong Shi San Hang

广州十三行诞生
The born of Guangdong Shi San Hang

康熙二十五年（1686年）至道光二十二年（1842年）的"广州十三行时期"，适值清朝的"康乾盛世"。那时，中国是世界经济最发达的国家，据统计，直至嘉庆二十五年（1820年）中国的GDP占世界经济总量的32.4%，居世界第一位；是世界最大的制造业国家，占据全球最大商品生产国宝座。在此时期，康熙皇帝于康熙二十三年（1684年）废除海禁、实行开海贸易政策和乾隆皇帝于乾隆二十二年（1757年）实行海路"广州一口通商"政策，清政府一方面希望继续通过海洋贸易赚钱，可又怕过度的贸易会导致社会体制动摇，这使广州成为中国唯一的对外贸易城市。十三行行商开始大步跨上舞台。

Guangdong Shi San Hang Period from 1686 to 1842 was during Kang-Qian prosperity. At that time, China was the most economical developed country in the world. According to statistics, until the twenty-five years (1820) China's GDP accounted for 32.4% of the world's total economy, ranking first in the world, and was the world's largest manufacturing country that occupied the world's largest commodity producing. During this period, Emperor Kangxi in Kangxi twenty-three years (1684) abolished the ban on the sea and began the sea trade. Emperor Qianlong in the twenty-two years of Qianlong (1757) began the implementation of the sea "Guangzhou a trade" policy. On the one hand, the Qing government hopes to continue to make money through the marine trade, but on the other, it was fear of excessive trade would lead to social system wavering. That situation made Guangzhou the only foreign trade city in China. Thirteen dealers began to step on the stage.

广州的海外贸易得以空前蓬勃发展，开辟了从广州出发，经澳门中转到全世界各国的8条国际航线：广州—澳门—果阿—里斯本—欧洲；广州—澳门—长崎；广州—澳门—马尼拉—墨西哥—巴西；广州—澳门—望加锡—帝汶；广州—澳门—纽约；广州—澳门—温哥华；广州—澳门—澳大利亚；广州—澳门—俄罗斯。广州成为贸易全球化的中心市场，全世界各国的商人和中国各省的商人都云集来广州做生意。1798年（嘉庆三年），瑞典人龙思泰（Andersy Ljungstedt）到广州就亲眼看见并记述这种情况，说："广州的位置和中国的政策，加上其他原因，使这座城市成为数额很大的国内外贸易舞台……中华帝国与西方各国之间的全部贸易，都以此地为中心。中国各地的产品，在这里都可以找到，东京、交趾支那、东方群岛、印度各港口、欧洲各国、南北美洲各国和太平洋诸岛等地的商品，都被运载到这里。"

广州"十三行街，为西洋诸国贸易之所"。广州成为"洋船争出是官商，十字门开向二洋；五丝八丝广缎好，银钱堆满十三行"的国际十大都会的第一大都会，使得美国马萨诸塞州、乔治亚州、俄克俄州下的县、市有以广州（canton）来命名者，可见广州在英国影响之广大。十三行成为清廷的"天子南库"；十三行行商成为富甲天下的豪商，其中怡和行商伍秉鉴位居世界首富，拥资2600万银两（相当于今天50亿美元）。而此时期，美国首富仅拥有700万美元。2001年，美国《亚洲华尔街日报》评伍氏为世界历史一千年来全球最富有的50富豪之一。

海外贸易的航道同时是文化交流的通道。随着广州海外贸易的空前蓬勃发展，中西文化亦在广州互相碰撞、互相交流、互相影响、互相渗透。在此中西文化交流的大潮中，作为在"中国近代史中关系最巨，以政治而言，行商有秉命封舱停市约束外人之行政权，又常为政府官吏之代表，外人一切请求陈述，均须有彼辈转达，是又有唯一之外交权；以经济而言，行商为对外贸易之独占者，外人不得与中国其他商人直接贸易"的十三行商人，顺应时代潮流，以中介人（或曰边缘人）的身份，游离于中西文化交流之间做出反应。他们既以儒化商人的身份保持中国传统文化，又敢于突破"天朝"传统的羁绊，解放思想，勇于领潮接纳西方文化，使具有近代意义的西方文化得以传入广州。

1. 康熙五十七年（1718年）两广总督杨琳关于十三行的奏折
Memorials of viceroy of Guangdong & Guangxi about Guangdong Shi San Hang in 1718

2. 两广总督接见英国使团（1794年）
Reception for British missions in 1794

3. 乾隆二十二年十一月初十日（1757年12月20日），乾隆皇帝关于洋船只许在广东收泊不得再赴浙省贸易的上谕。此上谕的颁布，标志着"一口通商"历史的开始
The issue of imperial edict of Emperor Qian Long on foreign ships in 1757, marked the start of Canton System

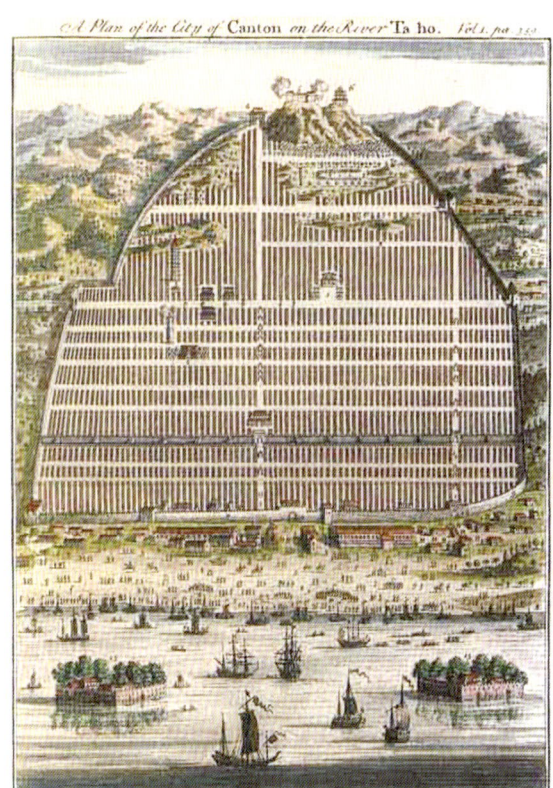

1. 康熙帝致罗马教廷的文件。罗马教廷认为中国人祭祖和拜孔子与天主教不能相容，禁止中国教徒祭拜祖先和孔子，康熙帝多次致书罗马教廷，抗议教皇对中国内政的粗暴干涉
The documents of Emperor Kangxi to Vatican

2. 广州城府图，这是清朝初期外国人绘画的广州城府图。图中描绘了珠江及岸上的热闹场景，并对衙门、炮台等重要建筑进行了数字标识
The map of Guangzhou city

蔚蓝船说——广东商船船型变迁

21世纪海上丝绸之路与广东航运丛书

1. 17世纪广州珠江和十三行景色
Guangzhou Pearl River and Shi San Hang in the 17th century

2. 清代珠江航运景观
Pearl River shipping landscape in the Qing Dynasty

3. 清代珠江景观
The pearl River landscape in the Qing Dynasty

4. 市舶司回府，这是一幅水彩画，画中描绘了市舶司到外国商船丈量货物征收税银，发给盖鉴后返回市舶司府衙的情景。大英博物馆藏有一卷完整无缺的相类似画作，全长26尺，绘于1760年
The Shibosi Back to the House, a water color painting

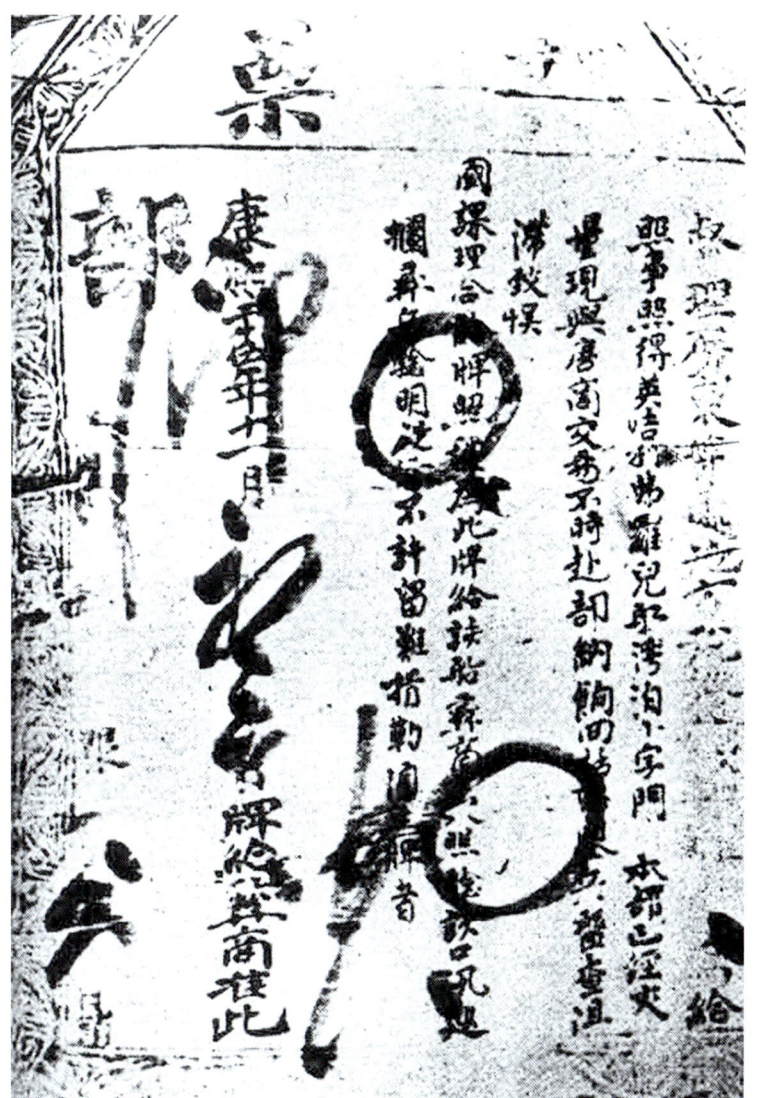

部票，这是康熙年间（1622—1722年）广东地方政府发给英国商船的部票，证明该船已经查验，不许留难指勒

The tickets given by Guangdong local government to British merchant ship to show its already checking status

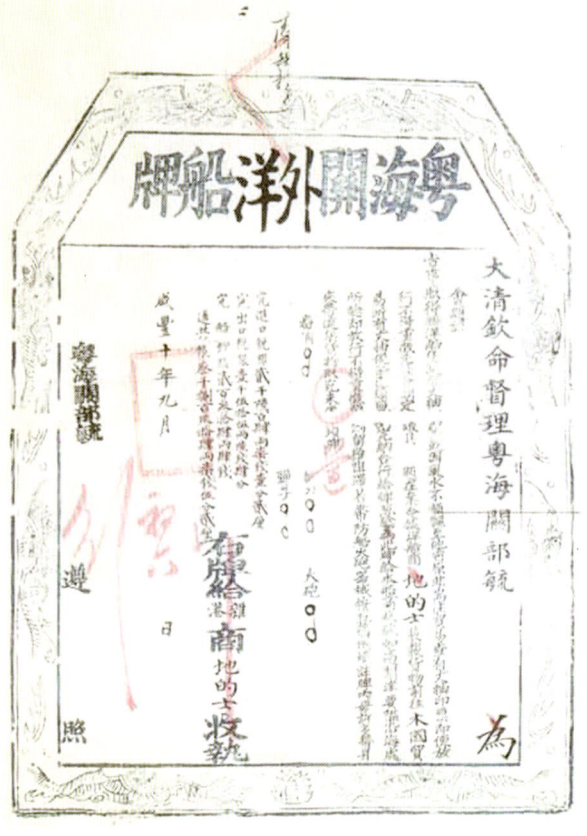

1. 粤海关外洋船牌，它是1745年粤海关颁发给瑞典王后号的航行中国的通行证
Guangdong Customs foreign ship card. It is awarded to the queen of Sweden in 1745 to the access to China

2. 海关官员在丈量船货。外国商船在黄埔湾泊后，粤海关便派员到船上丈量船货，收纳税款，商船再驶到广州商馆区对出的珠江，进行交易
The customs officer are measuring the cargoes

1. 粤海关，康熙二十四年（1685年），清政府宣布开海贸易，设粤、闽、浙、江四海关，标志着中国海关制度的开始。粤海关当时设广州城外的次固镇，地点在今起义路与泰康路交界处
Guangdong customs. Qing authority announced the marine trade to mark the beginning of China customs system

2. 右图位于黄埔湾的粤海关办事处。
Guangdong Customs Office

广州十三行辉煌史
Glorious history of Guangdong Shi San Hang

广州十三行，又称广东十三行、十三洋行，后来，这地区被称为"十三行街"，是源于清朝在广州设立的对外贸易特区内的十三家牙行商人：

伍秉鉴的怡和行，商名浩官，卢继光的广利行，商名茂官，

潘绍光的同孚行，商名正官，谢有仁的东兴行，商名鳌官，

梁丞禧的天宝行，商名经官，严启昌的兴泰行，商名孙青，

潘文涛的中和行，商名明官，马佐良的顺泰行，商名秀官，

潘文海的仁和行，商名海官，吴天垣的同顺行，商名爽官，

易元昌的学泰行，商名昆官，罗福泰的东昌行，商名林官，

容有光的安昌行，商名达官。

对于十三行的管理基本上是以官制商、以商制夷，并主要依靠两个制度：公行总商制度和保商连坐制度。公行总商制度就是在十三行商人中成立公行，类似于西方的行会。公行由粤海关任命总尚，进行广州对外贸易的一系列管理，承揽货税、裁定贸易商品价格。保商连坐制度来自于封建保甲制度，来广州做生意的外国商人必须有一位十三行商人作保商，出了什么麻烦责任由保商来负。

"如果我们在中国不受尊敬，那么我们在印度很快也会不受尊敬……如果我们会输掉这场战争，我们就无权开战；但如果我们打赢它，我们就无权放弃。"几分钟后，他给出了最后的结论："尽管令人遗憾，但我还是认为这场战争是正义的，而且也是必要的。"随即，大厅里响起了长时间的掌声。发表演讲的是一个叫托马斯·斯当东的英国人，他面对的是500多位英国下议院议员。这个当年曾在乾隆膝头玩耍，获赐槟榔荷包的孩子，此时已是个中国通。他那欧洲人所特有的对中国文明古国的梦早已破碎，现在他被虎门销烟所激怒，他相信枪炮是打开中国贸易封锁的唯一方式。

1840年，第一次鸦片战争爆发。英军军舰长驱直下，直接停泊在了南京的下关。清朝连忙派出钦差大臣，签下了中英《南京条约》，从此五口通商，十三行的外贸特权不复存在。随后道光二十三年七月初一（1843年7月27日）允许英国商人在各口岸任意与华商交易，广东丧失了在外贸方面的优势，广东十三行的辉煌时代也随之结束。

咸丰六年（1856年）第二次鸦片战争爆发，英军炮轰广州城。12月15日，城内市民愤怒烧毁十三行街，建筑物彻底化为灰烬，史称"西关大火""火烧十三行"。

1859年，英国人李泰国被委任为"中国总税务司"。7月，李在粤设立海关税务司，粤海关一切大权操控在英国人手上，同时确定了"值百抽五"的关税，粤海关连同中国其他海关税率被变相地固定在这一当时世界最低的税率标准上，英国人渴望了多年的"自由贸易"理念终于被灌输到了清帝国衰老的肌体里。十三行商馆从此彻底退出了中国对外通商贸易的舞台。

十三行行商与两淮盐商、山陕商人一同，被称为清代中国的三大商人集团。十三行行商和徽商晋商最大的不同就是十三行行商以海为根基的，什么都联系到海。中国贸易真正走向世界，是从十三行开始的。十三行标志了广东特有的历史地位，它的意义在于记录了广东在中国历史发展中的一段辉煌历程，在于广州自古成为中国最重要的商贸城市之一的标志和定位，对中国社会发展做出了重要贡献。十三行也体现了广东文化的一种精神，形成了以敢为人先、务实进取、创新发展、开放兼容为特质的区域文化传统，反映了中国社会发展的一种趋势。当同期的中国正走向一个以内陆性农业经济为基础的空前巩固的统一封建帝国的时候，以十三行为代表的开发性的海洋经济、海洋性社会组织和海洋性行为已经向海外扩展，在世界市场的形成过程中显示了自己的力量，对中国社会的发展产生一定影响。

虽然曾辉煌一时的十三行在两次鸦片战争之后完全消失，成为了历史陈迹，但却留下了丰富且具有价值的文化遗产。十三行商馆区是历史上广州密不可分的一部分，其展示的文化是清代广州文化的有机组成部分，也是当时广州社会的一个缩影。十三行的兴起和繁盛，反映了近代初期中西经济、文化互通互补的客观要求；表明了世界不同地区、不同民族之间可以通过和平交往、友好相处，达到互利共赢的目标；体现出粤商和岭南文化历来对外比较开放、兼容并蓄的特点，这是一个值得发扬的优秀传统；而十三行由盛至衰、终被毁弃的过程，也给了后人一个深刻的历史教训——只有顺应世界历史潮流、因时兴革，才是民族发展的正路。

1. 十三行近景
Close shot of Guangdong Shi San Hang

2. 十三行远眺
An overlook of Guangdong Shi San Hang

3. 1730年十三行
Guangdong Shi San Hang in 1730

1. 1780年油画描绘十三行的丹麦、西班牙、美国、瑞典、英国、荷兰夷馆
Painting depicts Thirteen 1780 for Denmark, Spain, Sweden, the UK, Holland, and American Yi guan

2. 1785年十三行
Guangdong Shi San Hang in 1785

3. 1796年十三行
Guangdong Shi San Hang in 1796

蔚蓝船说——广东商船船型变迁

21世纪海上丝绸之路与广东航运丛书 二

1. 1800年十三行
Guangdong Shi San Hang in 1800

2. 1805年十三行
Guangdong Shi San Hang in 1805

3. 1810年十三行
Guangdong Shi San Hang in 1810

4. 1820年十三行
Guangdong Shi San Hang in 1820

1. 1822年十三行大火初起的情景：天空上轮明月，商馆后街的中国楼房上火焰初升，居民们有的提着灯笼，有的挑着水桶前来救火，航艇上的人都指向了火场。画面漆黑，使人如置身布满浓烟的火场中
The fire of Guangdong Shi San Hang in 1822

2. 1822年十三行大火蔓延的情景：商行职员及水手前往灭火，但猛烈的火势把他们逼回船上，无奈地看着烈火燃烧。1822年广州十三行街大火，有四千万两白银化为乌有，史称"洋银熔入水沟，长至12里"
The fire was spreading of Guangdong Shi San Hang in 1822

蔚蓝船说——广东商船船型变迁

21世纪海上丝绸之路与广东航运丛书

1822年大火后十三行
Guangdong Shi San Hang after the fire in 1822

1. 1824年十三行
Guangdong Shi San Hang in 1824

2. 1825年十三行
Guangdong Shi San Hang in 1825

3. 1856年另一次大火后，此景已不复见。在画的左方，存艘侧轮蒸汽轮船，它是美国在中国的商贸代理旗昌洋行的"河鸟"号
Another fire in 1856

蔚蓝船说 —— 广东商船船型变迁

21世纪海上丝绸之路与广东航运丛书

1. 1844年美国花园
American Garden in 1844

2. 1848年美国花园
American Garden in 1848

1. 1850年十三行
Guangdong Shi San Hang in 1850

2. 从河南眺望十三行商馆。这幅水粉画前方是河南仓库区，挑夫正把一箱箱的茶叶运往舢板上，对岸是广州城的河堤，基督教堂清晰可见，它在1856年的大火中被烧毁。教堂前方泊碇了一艘汽轮船，是从美国波士顿来华的"火花"号
Looking at Guangdong Shi San Hang from Henan

1. 1856年十三行
Guangdong Shi San Hang in 1856

2. 十三行商馆前的货运码头
Wharf in front of Guangdong Shi San Hang

3. 十三行附近的市街，人头攒动，热闹非常，一位外国人正在选购中国漆器
The Street near to Guangdong Shi San Hang

1. 十三行同文街，这幅是石板画，作于19世纪
Slate of Guangdong Shi San Hang in the 19th century

2. 清代十三行靖远街入口处，作者海因，绘于1853年
The Qing Dynasty Shi San Hang Jingyuan Street entrance painted by Haiyin in 1853

3. 马戈尔尼使节团驶离虎门的情景。这是英国画家亚力山大于1796年画的水彩画。马戈尔尼是英国第一次派遣前往中国的使臣，亚历山大是马戈尔尼使节团的随团画家。此画原本的旧装裱上有如下记载：这是一幅珠江河口虎门的景色，马戈尔尼特使正在乘坐军舰狮子号往澳门，岸上的中国炮台鸣炮致敬
Scene of envoy Magorni left Humen. This is a watercolor painted by the British painter Alexandra in 1796. Magorni was the first British envoy sent to China, and Alexander was the accompanying painter of the Magorni envoy. This painting was originally recorded as follows: This is a picture of the Pearl River estuary Humen. Special envoy Magorni was to take the warships lion to Macau, when Chinese gun saluted at the shore

4. "古斯塔夫三"号，它是瑞典东印度公司最后一次派往广州的远征队船只之一
The Gustav No.3. is one of the ships that Swedish East India Company sent to Guangzhou last time

"哥德堡"号航行时的场景。"哥德堡"号是瑞典的商船,曾多次到中国,买回茶叶、丝绸、瓷器等货物。1745年"哥德堡"号回到故乡,在港口外触礁沉没。尽管商船沉没了,但拍卖打捞的货物,这次航行最终还是得到了14%的回报
The Goteborg

1. 载运英使之船即当时所称之英国贡船
Ship for carrying the British ambassador

2. 运载荷兰公司1655年的专使
Ship for carrying the Dutch ambassador in 1655

1. 黄埔帆影。这是一幅着色蚀刺版画，画面是从黄埔的长州岛眺望广州，图中描绘了往来河面的中外货船，左方的塔就是琶洲塔（1835年）
Sailing in Whampoa

2. 珠江上的海珠炮台。这幅水粉画描绘了海珠炮台及周边景色。海珠炮台筑于海珠石上，有祠庙，祭祀宋朝名宦李昂英，是古羊城八景之一，这里距商馆区仅一里之遥，是来穗外国画家最喜欢描绘的地方之一，1931年填海后，珠海石不复存在
Haizhu Battery in Pearl River

2. 林则徐虎门销烟图（1839年），林则徐把收缴英国和美国商人的二万多箱鸦片在虎门海滩销毁
Burning of Opium Stocks in Humen, 1839

下篇 广东航运文化

1. 1750年的牙雕广州港
The view of Guangzhou in 1750. This is a watercolor and gouache.The 1750 ivory carving of Guangzhou port

2. 1858年广州地图
The map of Guangzhou in 1858

3. 1859年广州
Guangzhou in 1859

第四章 珠江游船文化
Pearl River Cruise Culture

荔枝湾与艇仔粥
Litchi Bay and Sampan Congee

在清代的珠江水上，长期就有无数的小船在兜客，那时没有桥，河北河南只能借助小木艇往来。随着经济的发展，社会的开通，珠江开始有了各种游乐的小艇、大船。夜幕低垂，珠江边的黄沙和荔枝湾一带，花花绿绿的游乐船就要招客了。

历史上的荔枝湾，在驷马涌南之周门村，和象岗西面的芝兰湖（现广州市流花湖一带）相通，西至西场后注入珠江，"广袤三十余里"。是广州市历史悠久的风景名胜，素有"小秦淮"之称。

荔枝湾的历史可追溯到广州建城之初的2200多年以前。相传公元前206年，汉高祖刘邦派遣陆贾来广州向赵佗劝降，当时陆贾在今天的西村为驻地，筑泥城，并在河边种植花、藕和荔枝，开始经营这一名胜，"荔枝湾"因此得名。其后经过千百年来人工与天工的巧妙结合，成为广州著名的消夏游乐地。

南越国时，赵佗在今彩虹桥附近建越华馆（又称江浒楼）款待和迎送陆贾。张九龄诗《与王六履广州津亭晓望》，其《送广州周判官》诗有"海郡雄蛮落，津亭壮越台"句。唐代，建有著名的园林名胜"荔园"。南汉时，在泮塘建有华林园'又在今中山八路周门一带建有皇家园林昌华苑、显德园'在城北芝兰湖建有芳华苑、芳春园，"飞桥跨沼，桃花夹水一二里，林木夹杂如画"。每当荔熟之时，皇帝刘𬬭与宠妃臣子在苑中赏荔游乐，穷奢极欲，称"红云宴"。元时，荔枝湾西苑有柠檬园，所产柠檬用作元朝的贡品，口渴"摄里白"。位于洗马涌和上西关涌间的周门，至今仍有"西园地"及荔枝湾地名，表示唐、宋以来园林区所在。而芝兰湖旧址至今犹有"兰湖里"、流花桥等遗迹留存。

明代，荔枝湾为文人传颂，"一湾溪水绿，两岸荔枝红"，并以"荔湾渔唱"被列为羊城八景之一。清末，驷马涌畔的南岸村曾有蔡氏私人花园环翠园，占地2.3万平方米，以今环翠园街为主轴，铺砌有3米宽的白石路，两旁分建有船厅、意大利风格的玻璃厅和望云草堂等。园内一进三间的元善蔡公祠，占地4000多平方米，建筑用料精细，可媲美陈家祠，堪称广州生祠之最。

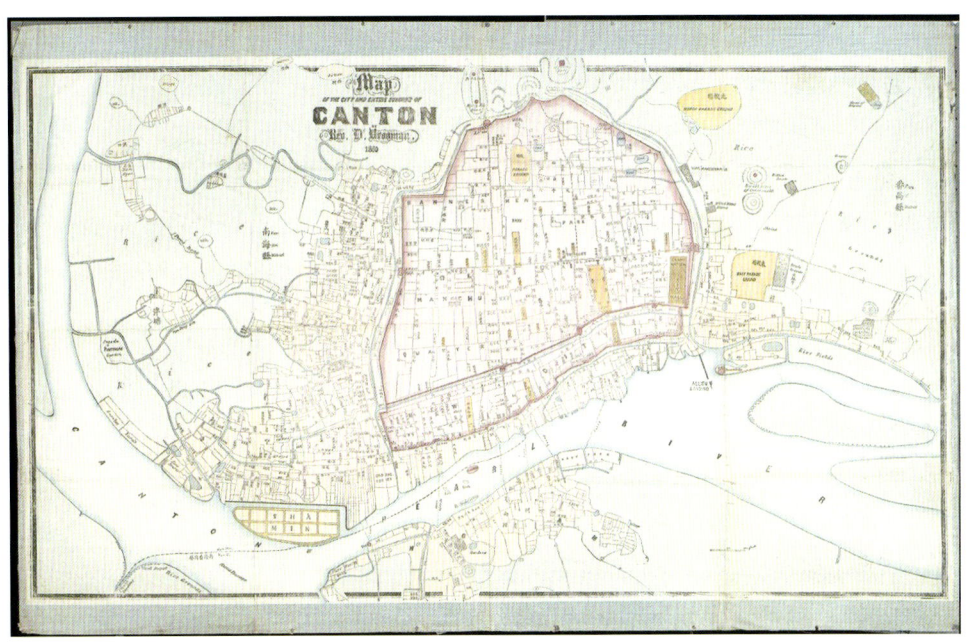

1860年广州地图中的旧荔枝湾
Map of Guangzhou at the old Litchi Bay in 1860

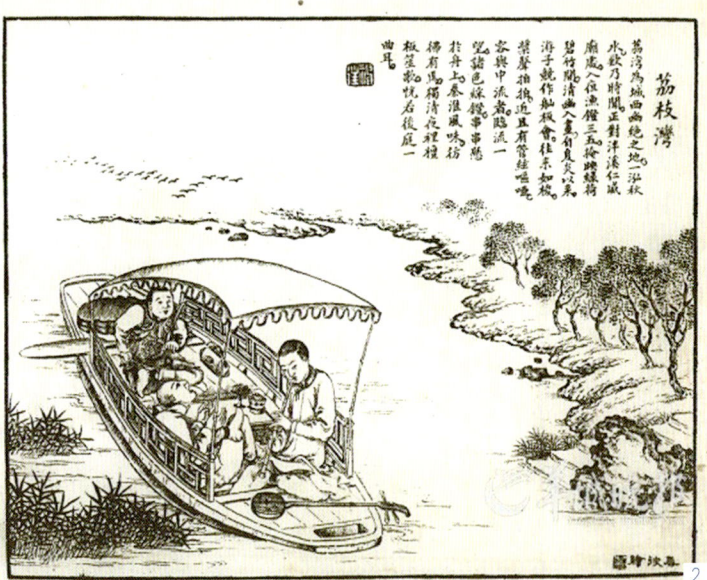

1. 环翠园老照片
Ring crest

2. 清末荔枝湾
Litchi Bay in late Qing Dynasty

1.民国时期的荔枝湾游河
Litchi Bay in the Republic of China

2. 现代荔枝湾
Litchi Bay today

艇仔粥是广东省广州地区著名的汉族小吃，广东粥品之一。以鱼片、炸花生等多种配料加在粥中而成。小虾香脆，鱼片、蛋丝软滑，鲜甜香美，适合众人口味。原为一些水上人家用小船在荔枝湾河、珠江边上贩卖，由于在艇仔上出售，故被称作"艇仔粥"，由于配料丰富，味道鲜美，深受大家欢迎。

1. 艇仔粥
Sampan Congee

2. 售卖艇仔粥的小艇
Boat for selling Sampan Congee

花艇与紫洞艇
Pleasure boats: Hua Boat and ZiDong Boat

花艇是指一种养有艺妓以娱乐宾客的船艇。船舱较为宽敞，可供歌舞，为当时珠江荔枝湾的特色。广州在中国历史上长期作为通商口岸，清代更成为国内唯一的通商口岸，商业气息浓厚，对外交往密切，生活方式染有浓重商埠色彩。广州水上人家当然也处于这种生态环境和生活方式中。他们以艇家之便，为当地居民和各方来客的生活消费需要提供方便。有专供食客吃喝的艇仔，其中就有驰名至今的"艇仔粥"。还有专供客人高档消费的"花艇"，艇仔装饰清雅秀丽，来客身坐艇中，一边临风品茗把酒，一边欣赏色艺双全艇妹的粤曲清音。花艇漂行江中，珠江两岸风光，岭南水域风情，荔枝湾那两岸的红荔，伴着一湾清水逶迤地流出珠江口，流向白鹅潭，荔湾河涌边的生活世态，尽收艇中旅客眼底。入夜，江面上花艇、画舫游弋其间，满江满湾，船火点点，加上艇仔粥的叫卖声，摇橹的欸乃声，丝竹弦乐声，粤讴俚歌声，使那江面热闹得可以和朱自清笔下的秦淮河媲美。

紫洞艇是清代一种流经广州城区珠江河段上的酒船，这种船上设有酒菜待客，有人陪酒，外省人称之为酒船。紫洞艇是平底木船，一般两层，下层可容纳四桌，二楼只容纳两桌，其余堆放杂物以及供船员住宿。新中国成立后，由于生活方式的改变，这种船逐渐消失。在番禺市沙湾镇的宝墨园，有一艘仿造古时紫洞艇建造的石舫。

花艇老图片
Pleasure boat: Hua Boat

1. 清末民初的花艇
Hua Boat in late Qing Dynasty

2. 旧广州的紫洞艇，可筵开几席
Zi Dong Boat in old Guangzhou

3. 花艇（1871—1874年）
Hua Boat, 1871-1874

1. 紫洞艇及花艇是旧日荔枝湾玩游地方
Pleasure boats in old Litchi Bay

2. 清末紫洞艇
Zi Dong Boat in late Qing Dynasty

3. 宝墨园仿古时紫洞艇建造的石舫
Zi Dong Boat Baomo Garden

4. 民国"游船消夏"
The "summer cruise" in the Republic of China

珠江夜游
Pearl River Night Cruise

珠江夜游从1960年7月1日就已经由市客轮公司开通了，那个时候没有专门的游船，游船都是由早上载客的渡轮"兼职"承担。一瓶啤酒、几颗花生，凉风习习，波涛阵阵，多年以前的"珠江夜游"属于木船上的回忆，清雅但却过于简朴。1981年，广州市客轮公司开辟西堤码头和天字码头到莲花山的旅游专线，1982年、1985年、1989年分别开辟西堤到金沙度假村、龙穴岛和横档岛的旅游专线。

20世纪90年代末，广东省珠江航运公司内河客运分公司和广州市客轮公司在传统的水上客运衰落之际，开始试探性地投入船只经营珠江游。目前，经营珠江日夜游的广州市客轮公司、蓝海豚、金航游轮公司等3家公司，拥有客位近6000余个。广州市客轮公司是老牌的航运公司，现拥有天字、西堤、芳村、中大等多座旅游专用码头轮渡码头33个，占全市码头的80%以上，有"信息时报"号"白鸥""花城明珠"等18艘各类豪华游船和2艘游艇，是广州市旅游码头及游船最多、规馍最大的珠江游公司。蓝海豚游船公司拥有"蓝海豚""牡丹卡"号"穗港之星"等5艘广州市最大、最漂亮、功能最齐全的大型豪华游船，还有1艘小型游艇"银海豚"和常规客船"贵华"轮。金航游轮有限公司拥有2艘大型豪华内河游船——具有岭南特色的"金舫"号和西式流行风格的"金璟"号，以及1艘豪华游艇"金鸥"号。如今，珠江游正逐步成为广州市引以为傲的一道旅游大餐。近些年来，珠江游客运量超过100万人次，由传统的水运向新型的珠江游转变。

珠江广州河段风光旖旎，两岸的名胜古迹和特色建筑物数不胜数：曾经主宰中国对外贸易的"十三行"、汇集世界各国古建筑风格的"沙面建筑群"、历经世纪风雨的"粤海关大楼""赤岗路""琶洲塔"依然伫立于珠江两岸。

江涛翻滚，游船从天字码头出发依次穿过海珠桥、海印桥、广州大桥、猎德大桥，那七彩的霓虹灯闪烁，让它们变成一条条跨江的彩虹，虹桥上车来车往，不禁让人疑惑：那，是否就是天上的街市？与珠江相拥而行的滨江大道和沿江大道上，如盖的绿荫丛被灯光折射，氤氲成一片幽幽的绿光，仿佛在细语母亲河的温柔与恩赐。江风飒飒，长堤上当然少不了相恋的伴侣，漫步的人们，在这样静谧的夜色中沉醉。他们，是珠江畔另一道美丽的风景。

船在江上行，十里花街十里灯，一幅幅动感灯画，或山水，或人物，或花鸟走兽，镶嵌在爱群大厦、海关钟楼、沙面的万国建筑等楼面上。光华流转间，时光仿佛也在倒流，远走的岁月和今天的摩登就这样完美地合二为一。南岸，半岛花园屋顶的绿色之冠在静静的夜空中闪烁，不远处中山大学北门的牌楼气势恢宏，"国立中山大学"的牌额，让人情不自禁地缅怀起一代伟人的风采。船依旧在游走。转过了白鹅潭，折向二沙岛，落入眼的是另一番美景："羊城八景"之鹅潭夜月、白天鹅展翅、星海音乐厅……

1. "信息时报"号，300客住三层游船，先后接待了多位国家领导人及多个国家的外国领导人
Information Times, a pleasure boat with a capacity of 300 seats has received a number of national leaders and foreign leaders

2. "广发证券"号，250客位双层游船，欧式风格
GF Securities, an European style pleasure boat with a capacity of 250 seats

1．"南海神·广州日报"号，总客位为268人，有"水上流动博物馆"之称
A ship with a capacity of 268 seats, is called "Flowing Museum"

2．蓝海豚，三层540客位，造型时尚
Blue Dolphin, a modern pleasure ship with a capacity of 540 seats

3．金舫号为290客位的游船，以欧洲游船的人性化特点、世界工业设计的最新设计潮流手法融合中国文化精华而创意设计出符合珠江文化特色的新型中式游船
Jin Fang, an innovative pleasure ship with a capacity of 290 seats

1. "小蛮腰"：高挑美人着"花衣"，广州塔乘船巡游，远远地就能看到纤细秀美的"小蛮腰"，像一个亭亭玉立的美人，顾影自怜地欣赏自己在珠江水面下投下的倩影
Canton Tower

2. 鹅潭夜月：白鹅潭又名"鹅潭夜月"，是羊城八景之一，其音韵悠扬的美景一直为人们所钟爱，可以说，"鹅潭夜月"是珠江夜游传统的保留观赏项目。入夜，清风送爽，月色溶溶。月光清辉倒映江中，与两岸灯火交相争辉。环顾四周，数座跨江大桥灯饰分明，白天鹅宾馆似少女沐浴江风，楚楚动人，"芳村花地"鸟语花香阵阵……身处此情此景，着实让人感叹——"此景只应天上有"
White Swan Hotel reflected on Pearl River at moon night is one of eight attractions in Guangzhou

3. 星海音乐厅：星海音乐厅的造型很特别，两个檐角高高翘起，加上明灭不定、色彩变幻的灯饰，它活脱脱是珠江边一只展翅欲飞的白天鹅
Xinghai Concert Hall

1. 粤海关大楼：有近百年历史的粤海关大楼，是广州作为历史上著名港口城市的标志性建筑。整个建筑带有浓郁的欧陆风情，令不少游客对其情有独钟
Guangdong Customs Building with a history of nearly 100 years

2. 天字码头：码头的名字就有"广州第一码头"之意，是广州目前使用时间最长的轮渡码头。在清代，天字码头是迎送过往官员的专用码头，如今，天字码头为市民提供过江和旅游之用。当年，林则徐曾在此登船前往虎门销烟，孙中山曾在此登船北伐……这个小小的码头见证了很多重要的历史瞬间
Tianzi Wharf

3. 中大码头：中大码头网为毗邻名校中山大学，是整段珠江夜游行程中人气最旺的路段。每晚，沿江路上满是悠闲散步、嬉戏的人群
Zhong Da Wharf is near to Sun Yat-sen University

第五章 轮船招商局在广东
China Merchants Steamship Navigation Company in Guangdong

  轮船招商局，1872年创立，总局设在上海，是自强运动中开办的第一家民用企业，其官督商办打破了晚清洋务企业纯粹官办的格局，首采股份制，也多为后世称道。在国内各大港口如天津、牛庄、烟台、汉口、福州、广州、香港以及国外的横滨、神户、吕宋、新加坡等处设立分局，从事客运和漕运等多项运输业务，为中国第一家近代轮船航运公司。

Steamship Merchant Steamship Company, founded in 1872, of which the General Administration was in Shanghai, was the first self-improvement campaign in the civil business. The government broke the pattern of foreign trade in the late Qing Dynasty. the first shareholding system, The In the major ports such as Tianjin, Niuzhuang, Yantai, Hankou, Fuzhou, Guangzhou, Hong Kong and foreign Yokohama, Kobe, Luzon, Singapore and other branches set up in passenger and water transport and other transport operations for China's first Home modern shipping company. It brought the first mining system, which is also praised by the later generations. Branches were set up in the major ports such as Tianjin, Niuzhuang, Yantai, Hankou, Fuzhou, Guangzhou, Hong Kong and foreign Yokohama, Kobe, Luzon, Singapore to operate passenger, water transport and other transport operations. It is China's first modern shipping company.

轮船招商局成立
The establishment of China Merchants Steamship Navigation Company

　　1867年在清政府总理衙门的通商口岸有不少商人购买或租雇洋船而又寄名在洋商名下，这种现象使清政府不得不开放购买或租雇洋船的禁令。清政府其实相当担心中国航运业会完全落入外国公司手中，以致遭粮输受制于人。因此总理衙门对当时容闳建议按西方公司章程，去筹组新式轮船企业，有相当大的戒心，这事一再延迟，直到李鸿章改以官督商办方式才成事。李鸿章在《论试办轮船招商》中说："目下既无官造商船在内，自无庸官商合办，应仍官督商办，由官总其大纲，察其利病，而听该商董等自立条议，悦服众商。"当时拥有政治实权的李鸿章得皇帝的许可，于1872年成立轮船招商局。

　　招商局成立后，在艰苦、险恶的环境中与外轮展开了激烈的竞争。在华的英国太古、怡和、美国旗昌等轮船公司，联成一气，采用大幅度降低运费等手段想挤垮招商局。李鸿章采取筹借官款、增拨漕粮及承运官物等措施，予以回击，使招商局转亏为盈。结果旗昌公司反遭破产，而太古、怡和等公司，不得不与招商局三次（分别为1877、1883、1889年）签订"齐价合同"：中外公司在各条航线上共同议定统一的价格，确定水脚收入和货源分配方案。从招商局讲，这具有打破外轮垄断中国航运业的积极意义，一定程度上保护了中国的权利。

李鸿章发起并创立招商局
Li Hongzhang founded the China Merchants Navigation Company

 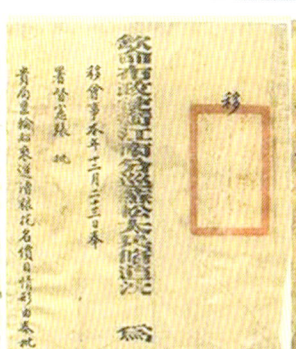 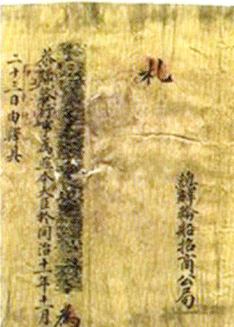 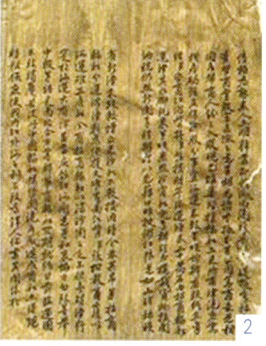

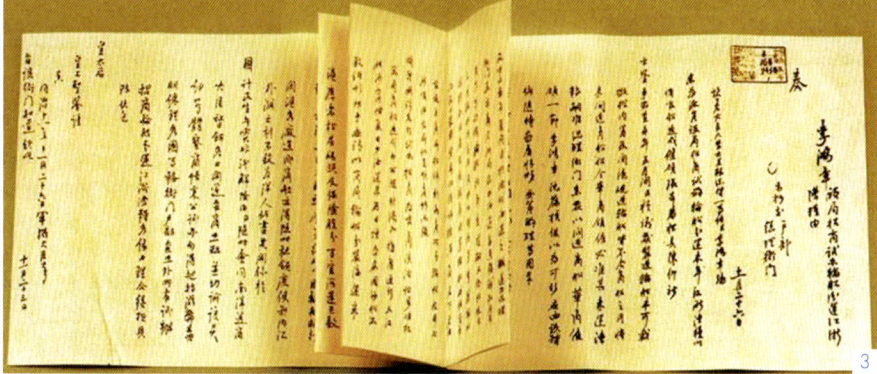

1. 上海外滩九号招商局旧址 （1901年）
China Merchants Steamship Navigation Company in Shanghai Bund, 1901

2. 1872年12月 23日，李鸿章奏请试办轮船招商局
On December 23, 1872, Li Hongzhang pled for trying running China Merchants Steamship Navigation Company

3. 1872年12月26日，清政府批准李鸿章提出的关于创立招商局的奏章《设局招商试办轮船分运江浙漕由》
On December 26, 1872, the Qing government approved the proposal of the memorial

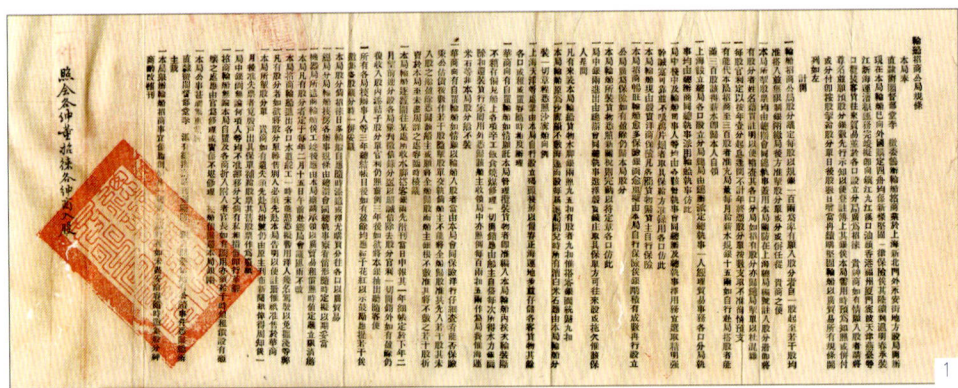

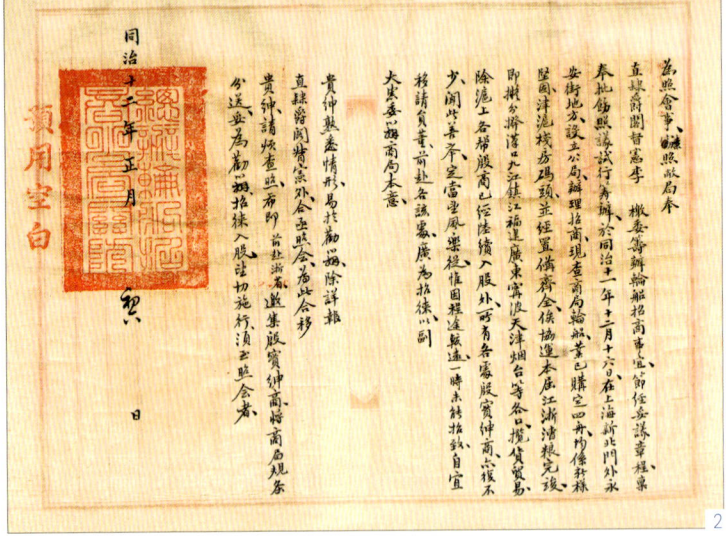

1. 招商局历史上的第一个章程——轮船招商公司规条（1872年12月）
Rules of China Merchants Steamship Navigation Company, the first constitution in its history

2. 招商局创办时的招股照会（1873年）
China Merchants Steamship Navigation Company founded the prospectus notes (1873)

"伊敦"号为1872年10月以50,397银两向大英轮船公司购得,排水量507总吨,载重一万担,航速11节,"伊敦"邮轮,航速快耗煤装载少,故停航于1877年5月拆卸改为囤船
Eton, a cruise ship purchased from British Shipping Company with a displacement of 507 tons, a carrying capacity of 10,000 tam, and a speed of 11 knots

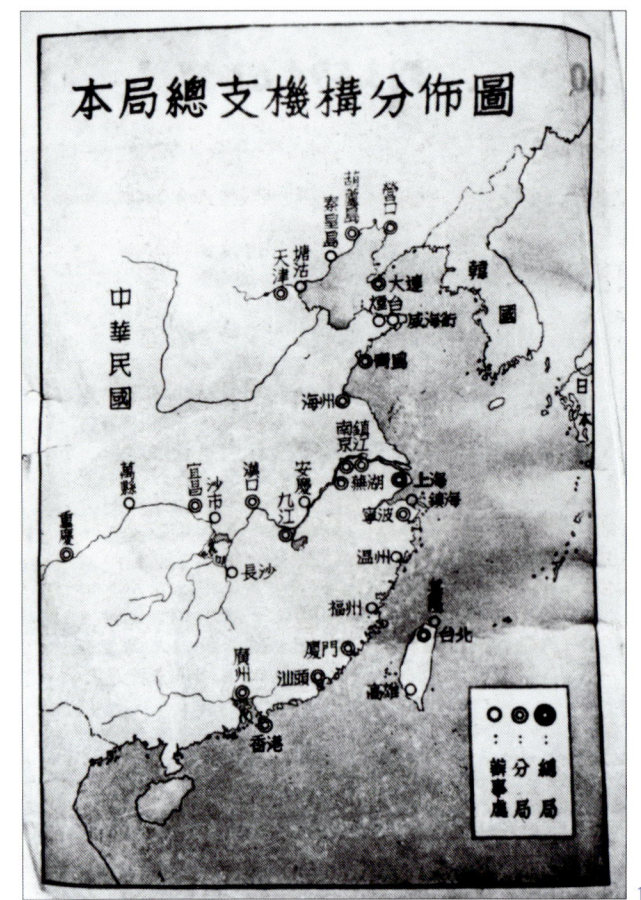

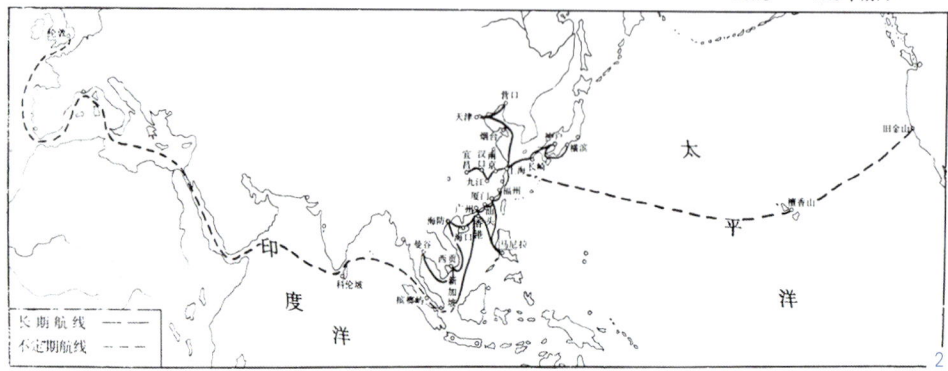

1. 招商局开局后,为了广泛开展业务,相继设立了19个分局,总分支机构,遍布中国沿海、长江
Expansion of business of China Merchants Steamship Navigation Company

2. 招商局创立后,迅速开辟了中国内河、沿海航线以及南亚、东亚、太平洋和大西洋航线
Expansion of ship routes of China Merchants Steamship Navigation Company

1. 招商局是中国近代最早,也是最大的民族航运企业。1881年,招商局投资建成中第一条专线铁路——唐山至胥各庄铁路
The first dedicated railway invested by China Merchant Steamship Company in 1881

2. 招商局开创了中国电讯业,1879年,招商局架设了中国人自己敷设的第一条专用电话线,为了沟通船岸联系,1929年5月18日,招商局还在上海首次设立船用无线电总台
China Telecommunication was established in China Merchant Steamship Company

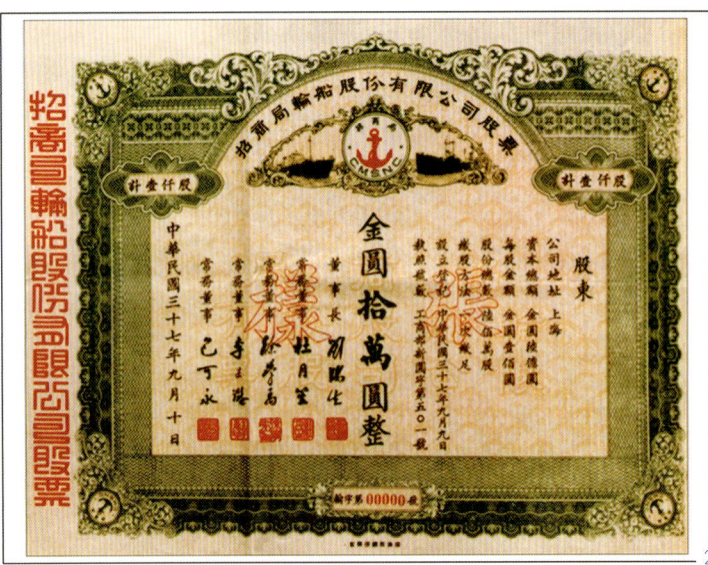

1. 1872年，招商局轮船运送的中国幼童赴美留学前在招商局大门前合影
In 1872, Chinese children were shipped to the United States to study. The photo was taken at the gate of China Merchants Steamship Navigation Company

2. 招商局是中国最早的股份制企业，在1873年创立时就实行了股份制，1948年发行的股票票样
China merchants Steamship Navigation Company is the earliest joint-stock enterprise, was founded in 1873. The stock sample issued in 1948

同治十二年元月十七日（1873年），招商局在上海南永安街正式封外开局营业。元月十九日，招商局从大英轮船公司购置的507吨的"伊敦"号货轮由上海装货首航香港，从此打通了中国沿海南北航线。

轮船招商局在广东
China Merchant Steamship Navigation Company in Guangdong

轮船招商局创立不久，便于同治十二年（1873年9月）在广州设立了分局。这是广州最早设立的海上运输机构，办公地点在广州六二三路186-188号。该分局在开始时业务一度比较清淡，但在唐廷枢兄弟经营下扭转局面，于1890年（光绪十六年）在广州置产，其后陆续在广州港添建码头，构筑货仓。

开办初期，招商局轮船以广州港为起讫点的航线有：（1）内河，光绪初年仅"安平"号轮行驶本港；（2）沿海，主要有5条：广州至牛庄、上海、汕头、香港、澳门；（3）远洋，招商局在开办初期，曾先后多次派轮船驶往日本长崎、神户、檀香山、吕宋、泰国、新加坡、印度、英国伦敦、海防等地，试图广辟远洋航线，扩大对外贸易；但因受外国资本主义势力以重征船钞、无理扣船等百般刁难，致使该局亏损甚大。到1882年，远洋航线仅存海防一处；1883年，因法国加紧侵略越南，战云弥漫，被迫宣告停航，至此，招商局开辟远洋航运的计划全部被破坏。

1932年，招商局广州分局由商办改为国营，从此即称"国营招商局广州分局"，直接由国民政府交通部管理。抗战时期，广州分局为抗战做出了重大贡献。抗日战争胜利后，招商局在国民政府的支持下恢复和新设业务机构，接收敌伪财产，购买美国、加拿大船舶，修复和新造码头仓库，恢复和新辟航线，新增油轮运输、船舶救捞等业务，合组经营远洋运输，在资产、规模和利润上达到了开局以来的顶峰。到1948年10月1日，国民政府为挽救统治危机开展币制改革，将招商局被组为招商局轮船股份有限公司，招商局在国内外设立的分公司、办事处、代理处共达43个，员工总数达到15,665人，船舶466艘。

此后广州分局由过去单纯代理上海总局业务，变为既代理业务又兼独立经营的航运机构。南北洋航线得到发展：1946年4月8日，招商局以"海鄂"轮首航上海—汕头—广州线，嗣后，"海皖""海康"两轮也加入该线行驶。是年，招商局广州分局"林森""培德""汉民""仲恺"轮航行广州—香港—上海线；"海粤"轮航行广州—厦门—上海线；"邓铿""延闾"轮航行广州—香港—上海—青岛—大连—天津线。远洋运输航线也有所增加。广州分局自身拥有的船舶主要用于内河驳运。

随后因国民党发动内战，招商局被迫参与繁重的军事运输任务，正常的经营被打断，结束了短暂的辉煌。1949年4月23日，中国人民解放军解放南京，招商局总公司开始随国民党军队、机关一起迁往台湾。撤至台湾的船只共计95艘，计24.6万吨，其中海轮（尤其是自由轮、大潮型轮、格莱型轮等性能较佳之巨型船舶）80艘，占原有海轮总数的81％。撤往台湾的人员总数为5,356人，大约占当时全局员工人数的三分之一。

1950年香港招商局及13艘海轮起义成功，成立护产委员和纠察队，与国民党派来的特务等展开了长达9个多月的惊心动魄的护产斗争。董华民带领全体起义员工、船员粉碎了敌特的种种阴谋，至10月18日，13艘起义海轮终于全部成功归航广州（"海玄"和"永灏"二轮因种种原因未能返回祖国），为新中国留下了一笔宝贵的财产。11月5日，周恩来总理发电报嘉勉汤传篪、陈天骏和全体起义员工。

1951年2月1日，招商局（上海总公司）改组为中国人民轮船总公司，并与交通部航务总局合并，其分支机构同时更名。旌帜仍沿用招商局第四面"红底黄月水波纹"局旗中的"红底""水波纹"，红底黄五星水波纹旗是招商局的第五面公司旗，是新中国唯一的一面与五星红旗标识相结合的公司旗帜。它体现了招商局在新中国航运事业中的地位，也是招商局与新中国休戚相关、命运与共的历史见证。

1979年，创办中国首个对外开放的蛇口工业区；1986年曾创办过中国第一家银行和保险公司的招商局，再次进军金融业，收购了香港友联银行，创中资企业收购香港上市公司的先例，并成为中国首家拥有银行的非金融性企业；1987年，招商局创办了中国大陆自1949年以来的第一家股份制商业银行——招商银行，成为中国银行业经营体制改革的起点。1988年，招商局倡导成立了中国大陆第一家由企业合股兴办的保险公司——中国平安保险公司，同时还收购了伦敦和香港的两家保险公司，成为第一家进入国际保险市场的中国企业。

现在的招商局集团是一家综合性的大型企业集团，经营着交通运输及相关基础设施建设、经营与服务（港口、公路、能源运输及物流、修船及海洋工程）、金融投资与管理、房地产开发与经营等三大核心产业。

1. 从利物浦购进"代勃来开"号，载重661吨，改名"永清"行驶上海广州香港（1885年）
 Bolai Lhe purchase from Liverpool with 661 tons, was later renamed as Yong Qing travelling to Shanghai, Guangzhou, and Hongkong routes (1885)

2. "安平"轮，排水量1.962吨，长80.8米，宽11.6米，深6.9米，吃水5米；蒸汽主机功率632千瓦，航速9.5节，日耗煤23吨；载客600人
An Ping was 80.8 meters long, 6.9 meters wide, 6.9 meters deep, and with a draft of 5 meters. The power of main steam turbine was 632 kW, and the speed was 9.6 knots, which cost 23 tons of coal every day. It has a capacity of 600 seats

3. "海鄂"（原名"Chippewa/建造：USA.1920"），大湖型商船为美国于1919年所建造的老船，排水量2.499.59吨，长度为77米，吃水6.9米，Scotch锅炉2具，三段膨胀式蒸汽主机一台，马力1,200匹，速率8节
Hai E (formerly known as the "Chippewa/Construction: USA. 1920", was a big lake-style merchant ship built by America in 1919. Its displacement was 2499.59 tons, and the length was 77 meters. It was equipped with 2 Scotch boilers, a 3-expansion main steam turbine, which gave it a power of 1200 horses and a speed of 8 knots

4. "海粤"（原名 "Norindies/建造：Saginaw. Mich.1920"），参数似"海鄂"
Hai Yue (formerly known as the" Norindies/: Saginaw Mich, 1920, the construction of "), the parameters like Hai E

1. "培德"（原名"Alfred M. Lunt/建造：New Orleans,1943"），纽奥良建造的浅吃水小型商轮，排水量1872.8至1925吨，载重约2800吨；长度86.3米，吃水5.7米；主机为单流双联蒸汽机，马力13000匹，航速11节，日耗油15吨
Pei De (formerly known as" Alfred M.Lunt/: New Orleans, built 1943 New Orleans") construction of the shallow draft and small business,a displacement of 1872.8 tons

2. "邓铿"（原名"Benjamin M. Melcher/建造：New Orleans,1943"），参数似"培德"
Deng Keng (formerly known as "Benjamin M. Melcher/ New Orleans, 1943 building:"), like Pei De

1.2.3.4. 1948年轮船招商局纪念邮票
China Merchants steamship Navigation Company commemorative stamps in 1948

1. 1948年8月30日，国营招商局接收新购"郑和"轮时中美双方人员合影
Zheng He, a new ship purchased by state-owned China Merchants steamship Navigation Company from the U.S. on August 30, 1948

2. 香港13艘起义海轮胜利归航广州，回到祖国的怀抱
13 ships of Hongkong returned to China with victory

汤传麓、陈天骏两位经理并转全体起义员工同志们：

你们在香港坚持了九个月的护产斗争，粉碎了帝国主义和蒋介石匪帮的一切迫害和阻挠，终于胜利地将全部起义的轮船驶回人民的祖国。你们英勇不屈斗争，在维护祖国财产和发展人民航运事业上，是有很大贡献的。尚望努力学习，为进一步发展人民的航运事业而奋斗。

周恩来
十一月五日

1. 周恩来总理贺电
Congratulatory message from Chinese premier Zhou Enlai

2.1949年9月19日，招商局"海辽"轮在船长方枕流的率领下，由香港秘密辗转到达巴林海峡宣布起义，他们巧妙伪装船身，躲过国民党飞机、军舰和电台的侦察，经过9天9夜的惊险航行，安全抵达解放区大连港
Hai Liao, a ship of China Merchant Steamship Naviation Company in 1949

毛主席電賀起義的海遼輪全體人員

——新華社北京一九四九年十月廿四日電——

海遼輪方枕流船長和全體船員同志們：

祝賀你們在海上起義，並將海遼輪駛達東北港口的成功。你們為著人民國家的利益，團結一致，戰勝困難，脫離反動派而站在人民方面，這種舉動，是全國人民所歡迎的。是還在國民黨反動派和官僚資本控制下的一切船長、船員們所應當效法的。

毛澤東

一九四九年十月二十四日

1

2

3

1. 1949年10月24日，毛主席发电报给方枕流和全体船员，对起义义举表示祝贺
On October 24, 1949, Chairman Mao sent a telegram to Zhenliu Fang and the crew to extend congratulations on the uprising

2. 为纪念"海辽"轮起义回归祖国，新中国的货币上印有"海辽"轮图样
To commemorate the Hai Liao uprising's return to the motherland, the new Chinese currency printed with Hai Liao pattern

3. 1950年1月，香港起义归来"民302"轮全体船员
All crew of Min 302 returned from Hongkong in January, 1950

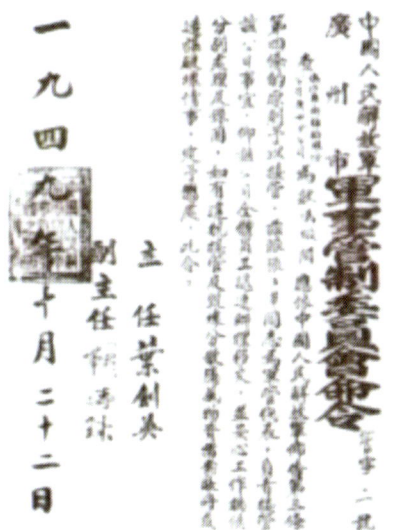

1. 1949年10月22日,广州市军管会关于接管招商局轮船股份有限公司广州分公司命令
An order from Guangzhou Military of taking over Guangzhou branch company of Guangdong Merchant Steamship Limited Co.

2. 广州海运局——1949年10月12日,广州解放,广州军管会接管招商局广州分公司,随后演变成华南区海运管理局,又演变成广州海运局
Guangzhou Maritime Bureau in 1949

蔚蓝船说——广东商船船型变迁

1. 招商局第一面旗
The first flag of China Merchants Steamship Navigation Company

2. 招商局的第四面旗子——国营招商局旗帜
The forth flag of China Merchants Steamship Navigation Company

3. 中国舰船旗帜
The Chinese people shipping flag

4. 位于香港维多利亚湾的招商局大厦—招商局集团总部
China merchants Group Headquarters is located in China Merchants Building of Victoria Harbor, Hongkong

1. 1979年7月，蛇口工业区基础工程正式破土动工，响起开山第一炮
In 1979 July, Shekou Industrial Zone infrastructure project officially started, first shot rang out first

2. 1984年1月26日，邓小平视察蛇口工业区
On January 26, 1984, Deng xiaoping visited the Shekou Industrial Zone

1. 招商局开发建设蛇口三十余年，蛇口由荒芜落后的小渔村发展成为美丽的海滨花园城
Shekou has been developed and constructed by China Merchants Steamship Company for over 30 years, changing from the barren and backward small fishing village into a beautiful coastal garden city

2. 招商局拥有目前中国最大的超级油轮船队
China Merchants Steamship Company currently owns the largest China super tanker fleet